Pay-Per-Click Search Engine Marketing Handbook

Low Cost Strategies for Attracting New Customers Using Google, MSN, Yahoo! & Other Search Engines

Boris Mordkovich • Eugene Mordkovich

MordComm, Inc.

Brooklyn, New York

This publication contains the authors' opinions and is designed to provide accurate and authoritative information. It is sold with the understanding that the authors are not engaged in rendering legal, accounting, investment planning, or other professional advice. The reader should seek the services of a qualified professional for such advice; the authors and publisher cannot be held responsible for any loss incurred as a result of specific investments or planning decisions made by the reader.

Edited by **Frances Krug**
Cover design by **David Gagne**
Screenshots by **Jonathan Limoanco**

ISBN: 978-1-4116-2817-5 | Printed in the United States of America | Third Printing

Dedicated to Our Family

Table of Contents

Chapter 1 – Introduction

Despite the ever-increasing presence of the Internet in almost every form of human communication, many businesses remain reluctant to become involved in paying to advertise products or services on the Internet, or are still unaware that online advertising is a viable option. Reasons for this reluctance are different for each business, but some of the major concerns expressed include:

♦ A belief that having a website listed on search engines is all that is needed for customers to find that website easily.

♦ A belief that potential customers do not like or trust paid advertising on the Internet and will visit only websites that come up in the "natural" or "organic" search results pages of a search engine such as Google.

♦ A fear of wasting marketing funds, due to a lack of knowledge of the paid advertising marketplace or unfamiliarity with the pros and cons of the various options available.

♦ A reluctance to become involved in managing online ad campaigns (in addition to existing traditional advertising campaigns) because of time constraints.

♦ The lack of a website and no plans to build one, so the Internet is not seen as a viable option for effective and affordable advertising.

♦ A perceived (or actual) lack of knowledge about computers and the Internet, leading to concerns that advertising on the Internet would be too complicated to set up and manage.

Of course, many other reasons can cause a business to bypass an online advertising opportunity. Some of the concerns are indeed valid and should be considered carefully.

In the past, paid advertising on the Internet was sometimes viewed as a desperate move by a failing company to sell its products or services; this view has been inaccurate for many years (if that perception was indeed ever valid). Now, paid Internet advertising is the most popular advertising method and the fastest-growing trend for businesses seeking to extend their market reach.

Within the various choices businesses have for including paid advertising in their marketing budget, the most popular by far is a type of online advertising called "pay per click."

At its most basic level, the premise of the pay-per-click ad is that the advertiser does not pay anything for the ad until someone actually clicks on it and is directed to the advertiser's website. These ads are typically more prominently displayed than regular search results and are often called "sponsored links."

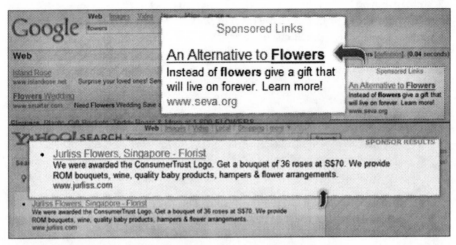

Figure 1.1 – Pay-per-click ads appear on popular search engines, such as Yahoo! and Google, alongside or above regular (organic) listings.

The concept of pay per click has been around since businesses began building websites and search engines gained popularity. However, this type of online advertising in its current form debuted in 1997, when an entrepreneur named Bill Gross developed an idea for the first-ever PPC search engine—GoTo.com (the name was changed to Overture in 2001 and the company was acquired by Yahoo! in 2003).

Ironically, people were quite skeptical of the idea in its early days, feeling that nobody would choose to use a search engine filled with ads. It wasn't until late in 2000, when Google introduced their Google AdWords program, that the pay-per-click industry began to mature.

In the years since 2000, pay per click has evolved into a very diverse and widely used method of online advertising. It also spawned a complex support industry, with numerous businesses creating software and other tools to help advertisers craft better advertising and more easily manage their ad campaigns.

Because the concept of pay-per-click advertising on the Internet is relatively new to businesses with (or without) an online presence, and is in a constant state of development, we decided to write this book to explain all aspects of pay-per-click advertising to those who want to take advantage of it.

Any business can benefit from this type of advertising—from companies without a website, to those with an online presence who have never heard of pay-per-click advertising.

Advantages of Reading the "Pay-Per-Click Search Engine Marketing Handbook"

This book is, in many ways, the culmination of knowledge we have accumulated over the past several years of observation and participation in e-commerce. We have seen the potential of pay-per-click advertising grow enormously through the last few years, exceeding even the most optimistic expectations of many online experts.

We wrote this book to help business owners—especially those operating small-to-medium-sized businesses—understand pay-per-click advertising and then use it to their advantage. By reading and following the procedures in this book, and carefully considering the relevancy of the available advertising venues we discuss in terms of your own products or services, any business owner will be able to compete effectively in the pay-per-click advertising world.

Why use pay per click over the other types of online advertising available?

The growth of the online advertising industry makes pay-per-click advertising the most popular and lucrative means of online advertising today. Variations of the standard advertising model are being developed, marketed, and used by large companies already firmly entrenched online and well aware of how pay per click works. Meanwhile, the majority of business owners, especially those with smaller businesses, may still struggle to understand the basics of these techniques.

Pay per click is on the rise in the online game, and we agree with research groups, such as The Kelsey Group, that it will be a viable option for advertising dollars for quite some time, even though changes to the traditional model will continue to evolve as time progresses.

If you are a business owner who wishes to increase online visibility and ensure prominence on the first page of search results, the opportunities offered by the pay-per-click model of advertising cannot be overlooked. It is an option you need to become fully informed about in order to compete effectively in today's marketplace. Online advertising, if properly managed and created with knowledge and foresight, can draw huge numbers of potential customers to your website—prospects who are already interested in the product/service you offer.

To take advantage of the pay-per-click advertising model, you need to know how to set up and maintain an ad campaign. This book will provide you with all the information you'll require.

We cover the basics of pay-per-click advertising as well as facts that few people, outside of those with an enormous amount of experience running pay-per-click advertising campaigns, know. These facts can help you fine-tune your advertising.

We provide you with reviews of all kinds of search engines that offer pay-per-click advertising programs and advice on how to get the most out of your online advertising dollars. We've also reviewed software and online tools that will help you manage and optimize your pay-per-click advertising campaigns.

We've even included tips from some of the top experts in the field featuring little-known techniques that can increase the effectiveness of your pay-per-click ads.

Many businesses haven't taken advantage of this powerful form of online advertising because it is relatively new, the terminology is quite technical, and the process can be confusing—in short, because they simply don't know where to start!

In addition to helping you understand the process, we present a general overview and detailed instructions on how to set up a pay-per-click ad campaign. Then we address more complex matters such as click fraud, localized search, and contextual advertising, in order to help put you on the road to your first effective pay-per-click ad campaign.

We recommend that you read this book cover to cover, and then keep it close by so you can refer to it as questions arise in the future.

Although this book is targeted at those readers who do not have much experience with pay-per-click advertising (or have never heard of this advertising method), experienced marketers will find useful, interesting, and relevant tips as well.

The online advertising industry is constantly changing, so we intend to publish an updated version of this book every year to reflect changes to pay-per-click programs and to discuss any trends that may challenge the popularity of these programs.

Right now, however, pay per click can be the easiest and often even the cheapest way to advertise online. Used correctly, it can turn visitors to your website into buyers of your products or services.

That is the ultimate purpose of this book—to provide you with the knowledge you need to set up a pay-per-click advertising campaign that will work for you and your business. We invite you to turn the page and take the first step towards succeeding in your online business ventures.

Chapter 2 – What is Pay-Per-Click Search Engine Advertising?

Because its popularity is relatively recent, some business owners neither understand what "pay-per-click search engine advertising" means, nor do they realize its enormous potential for increasing their online presence and bringing more traffic to their websites. Even those who understand basic search engine marketing techniques sometimes fail to make the distinction between a pay-per-click (hereafter, PPC) ad campaign and organic search engine optimization (see the Glossary in Appendix 1 for a definition of this and other terms).

The purpose of this chapter is to:

♦ Clarify the basic operation of a PPC ad campaign

♦ Provide some major highlights of the development of PPC advertising

♦ Compare the primary differences between PPC advertising techniques and search engine optimization

How Pay-Per-Click Search Engine Advertising Works

Pay per click (PPC) is the placement of a small "ad" on the search results page for a specific keyword or keywords in return for a specified payment when a visitor actually clicks on that ad.

Keep in mind that the advertiser pays nothing to appear on the results page per se; they only pay the amount they have agreed to (or bid for) when someone actually clicks on their ad and is taken to the "landing" page on their website. Therefore, the term "pay per click" means just what it says: the advertiser pays each time a visitor clicks on their ad.

The first step in putting together a PPC campaign is to decide your budget and the level of risk you are willing to take. Both aspects will help determine which PPC search engine(s) you ultimately choose to start with. As one would expect, the larger search engines are less risky endeavors, because they already have excellent market coverage and tend to offer a lot of assistance to their users. However, they also are the most expensive in terms of how much money you must spend to acquire a visible ranking.

The second step is to choose your keywords. There are plenty of free, independent tools available to help you research keywords. Many of them will also tell you the current bid price for certain words or phrases on different search engines. (Later in this book you will find a review of a number of the leading tools available.)

The third step is to compose two things: the headline that will appear on the search results page, and a description of your product or service, or other promotional text. Descriptions are usually limited to 200 characters or less and should contain your chosen keywords.

Some PPC search engines strictly control the text that can appear in the listing and manually review each advertisement; others are more lenient and approve ads more or less automatically.

Next, you must open an account with a PPC search engine. Be prepared to supply your name, company name, address, phone number, email address, and so on. As a rule, opening an account is free. You will not be charged until you have bid on the search words you want and have funded your account.

You will also be given a number of alternatives for funding your ad campaign. For instance, you may fund your account with a credit card for a set amount, such as $100. When this amount is exhausted, all advertising stops. Alternatively, you may be able to set a monthly spend limit where your ad will no longer appear once the limit is reached. Carefully consider the consequences of the funding option you choose to avoid unanticipated draws on your credit.

In general, the initial deposit for a PPC ad campaign varies between $25 and $50. Some search engines will even give you a nominal amount of money as a bonus to begin your campaign with.

Be sure to read the fine print in the agreement to be clear on minimum deposits required, as well as what happens to your deposit if you decide to cancel your campaign.

Now you can begin bidding for keywords.

When you first register the keywords you have chosen with the search engine (and some large businesses will have thousands of keywords), you must specify the maximum amount you are willing to bid for those keywords.

The price of a keyword can range anywhere from 1 cent to a few dollars or more, depending on its popularity as a search term and the search engine itself. Naturally, advertisers who pay more appear higher on the search results pages.

Depending on the industry, you may find that there is fierce competition between advertisers for popular keyword(s). The business that bids the highest amount of money for a specific keyword will be ranked first in the PPC results, the second-highest bidder will be ranked second, etc.

Typically, search engines limit the number of paid ads on a results page to fewer than 10, and research has shown that the first five PPC ads generally get the majority of the visitors (hits).

Furthermore, the top three listings usually get the most exposure, as they are syndicated throughout the search engine's partner network.

Is a Pay-Per-Click Campaign the Right Investment for My Business?

Pay-per-click advertising is generally considered an excellent way to advertise your business online. It is relatively easy to set up and inexpensive as well.

Search engines offer varying amounts of support, and some are easier to use than others, but the opportunity to ensure placement of your ad without investing a large number of marketing dollars makes PPC an extremely attractive option. As a business owner, you should not ignore this potent marketing technique!

Pay Per Click Versus Search Engine Optimization

Many people have difficulty understanding the different parts of search engine marketing (SEM).

In a nutshell, SEM consists of two completely different techniques:

- ◆ SEO (search engine optimization), and
- ◆ PPC (pay-per-click advertising) and other paid advertising programs.

Although this book is meant to educate you about PPC advertising, we feel it's important that you understand what regular search engine optimization is.

SEO is the process of preparing your website and its constituent pages for prime positioning on search engines using specific keywords. SEO is actually very complex, as key parameters change on a regular basis and continuing maintenance and application of those parameters to maintain search engine position can be very time-consuming.

If you want to learn more about it, a good place to start is www.searchenginewatch.com. In addition, the website for our publication "Search Marketing Standard" magazine (www.searchmarketingstandard.com) is also a prime resource for all aspects of both SEO and PPC.

If you want to outsource your SEO program to a professional, we recommend that you check out www.seo-guy.com for suggested agencies.

Some website owners believe that SEO and pay per click are the same process, perhaps because both involve search engines. However, they are completely different and independent types of marketing.

Let's look into some of the main differences between SEO and PPC.

1. **Purpose**—both SEO and PPC are designed to attract traffic via search engines.

    > **Search Engine Optimization**—to appear as near the top as possible in the organic (or natural) search results for keywords relevant to your website.

    > **Pay Per Click**—to instantly attract qualified prospects and leads to your website and convert them into buyers.

2. **Keywords**

    > **Search Engine Optimization**—one usually wants to target general terms, as they provide the most amount of traffic.

    > You don't always have complete control over which keywords will be chosen to decide a rank for your site, nor do you have any control over the ranking you will receive.

    > **Pay Per Click**—you have complete control over which keywords are used and their position on the search results page. You can change the actual ad, as well as set up different ads for different keywords. More specific keywords lead to higher-quality visitors than do general keywords.

3. **End Result**

    > **Search Engine Optimization**—depending on your keywords and the resulting ranking you receive in the search engine, you attract free traffic to your website.

    > **Pay Per Click**—you pay for each visitor you receive, but you can control the number of visitors you get, the landing page to which they are directed, the keywords being used, and other important factors.

As you can see, the two processes are quite different in techniques, methods, and execution, but the desired end result is the same—to receive quality traffic from search engines. With SEO, you have less control and are dependent upon your site meeting each search engine's specific rules. With PPC, you can control every aspect of your campaign.

The Popularity of Pay-Per-Click Advertising

Let's conclude this chapter with a consideration of the popularity of PPC in terms of searchers and advertisers.

Recent surveys of trends in the Internet marketplace show that a majority of people in some key demographic groups are increasingly using the Internet, not just to research products, but also to buy them.

> Some products tend to be researched but not purchased online, such as large appliances, but with local search options, even in those instances, one can benefit from online advertising.

Results of a survey by The Kelsey Group, which were announced in February 2004, showed that:

◆ Of the 5,582 people surveyed who had made one or more purchases on the Internet in the previous year, 64% used search engines to find what they were looking for.

◆ One-third of all searches were done for shopping purposes (which includes looking for a seller, researching a possible purchase, or actually purchasing something online).

◆ Almost half of the respondents (44%) reported performing more commercially based searches than in the previous 12-month period.

Keep in mind that these percentages come from a statistically significant group of people who were already proven online buyers.

In the time period since The Kelsey Group's 2004 study, PPC advertising has grown significantly in usage and many refinements and enhancements to crafting a PPC advertising campaign have been made based on continuing market research. With such constant change, it is difficult to offer more than some "snapshots" of trends in PPC through 2006.

For example, a September 2006 study released by WebSideStory suggested that the median order conversion rates between paid search and organic search were very close—3.40% for paid search and 3.13% for organic search. Sample size and methodology, however, indicated the study was based on "more than 57 million search engine visits to nearly 20 major business-to-consumer e-commerce sites .... These sites generate an estimated $2.5 billion per year in online sales. Order conversions occurred during the same sessions." (Source: WebSideStory Press Release dated September 22, 2006)

Thus, although an interesting study by a reliable and respected source, potential advertisers need to take note that the study involved fewer than 20 websites with very high online sales numbers. This is not a study highlighting sales of the type or scale typical of small-to-medium-sized businesses operating on the Internet.

However, though the face of PPC advertising has become more complex in the last year—involving contextual, behavioral, geo-targeting, day-parting, niche marketing, viral marketing, social search, mobile search, etc.—some trends can be perceived.

A study released by comScore Networks at the end of March 2006 reported that 63% of purchases tied to online search during the holiday sales season in late 2005 took place offline. That means that 37% of buyers converted online. The study relied on data from 832 million Americans and 552 million searches over 11 product categories and 24 different search engines.

James Lamberti, VP of comScore Search Marketing Solutions stated, "it's clear from this study that the influence of search on offline buying can often be responsible for the major portion of the overall financial return from investments in search marketing." (Source: Press release from comScore dated March 21, 2006)

Other studies support the increasing importance of search, and particularly paid search, in consumer purchasing decisions. Perhaps the most significant finding targeting paid search was Marketing Sherpa's conclusion that, for the first time in three years, paid search was rated the best performing online marketing tactic (in a survey of 680 marketers who spend an average of 44% of ad budgets online throughout 2005 in Marketing Sherpa's "Best and Worst Tactics of 2005" study).

Given that more consumers are looking online for information on purchases and are making more purchases online than ever before, combined with recent studies indicating that searches still rarely go beyond the first three pages of organic search results (an example being the iProspect Search Engine User Behavior Study of April 2006), engaging the user early on takes on even more importance. The highly relevant PPC ads results on the first search engine results pages (SERPs) can be a prime source for conversions and sales.

The next chapter continues this discussion in more detail, providing more information on why advertisers should use pay-per-click advertising instead of, or in addition to, the marketing methods they already use.

Chapter 3 – Why Use Pay-Per-Click Advertising?

Combining Pay Per Click With Search Engine Optimization

It may seem that, if conducted properly and thoroughly, search engine optimization (SEO) is all you need to guarantee a top-ranking position in search engine results.

Sadly, that is not the case. Even using the best SEO techniques, your listing is at the mercy of the search engines in terms of where it is eventually placed. Even though you may have followed all the suggestions, and placed keywords in the proper density and places, once you submit your website you must wait until the next spider crawl before your site will be (hopefully) added to the index of pages on the Internet. Quite possibly, you will be vying with dozens of competitors for the same top positions. Even once you are listed on the search engines, you must continually tweak your SEO campaign to hold on to or improve your ranking.

One continuing concern raised by webmasters in online forums is that the ranking of their site keeps changing, even though they have not made any changes to their site. Many factors can be responsible, but don't forget to keep in mind that new sites may have been found during the latest crawl that the search engine considers more relevant—a key component spiders use in deciding the ranking order of websites.

To sum up:

- SEO is an extremely important part of online marketing because, when done well, it can ensure good organic rankings in search engines.

- SEO is only one part of a successful online marketing campaign.

- It can take quite some time for your site to show up on search results, and you have no absolute control over its ranking position.

- Without a component that ensures placement on the first page of search results, you risk not reaching your potential audience.

The Effect of Ad Location on Reader Response

A number of studies conducted in the past couple of years have tracked how users read (or scan) the content on web pages. Studies have consistently shown that people typically begin looking at the information in the upper-left quadrant of a web page and then track left to right across the page. Their gaze then usually returns to the left side of the page, scanning the content as they swing back to the left, and viewers finish by looking down the left side of the page.

Some studies place emphasis on this so-called "Golden Triangle" (an inverted pyramid shape starting in the upper-left quadrant that may or may not extend to include the area in the right-hand side column where PPC ads are often placed); others claim viewers move more in an "F" shape (left to right horizontally, down and swinging back to the left column and then down the page).

> Pay-per-click ads are generally located to the right of the organic listings (or on top of them) in a section called "sponsored links" or similar terminology.

With PPC ads located at the top of organic listings, as well as usually "above the fold" (in the part of the page viewable without having to scroll) on the right side of the page, they are in good position to be among the first items viewers see and are influenced by.

Another consistent finding over the past few years of research is that viewers rarely look beyond three pages of organic listings resulting from a search request, and the majority don't venture past the first page (usually about 10 listings). Therefore, unless your SEO efforts result in placement of your listing in the first page of results of a user's search, realistically you have a relatively small chance of being seen by potential clients.

For these and other reasons, ensuring maximum exposure requires more than just relying on SEO and submission to search engines. You must also consider pay-per-click advertising, which complements and builds upon elements of SEO in a way that many other advertising methods do not.

The Advantages of Combining Pay Per Click With SEO

What advantages are there to using pay-per-click ads with search engine optimization to enhance visibility of your website?

♦ PPC requires a relatively small investment, so companies can determine the effect keywords and landing pages have on visitor behavior before investing larger amounts of their budget in SEO.

♦ Information about your products or services appears in front of users almost immediately. With PPC, you can literally start getting targeted visitors, leads, and sales in a matter of hours.

- ◆ PPC ads are usually placed in a prominent position right next to (or just above) the organic search engine results. Thus, the ad is right in front of the searcher and likely to be seen.

- ◆ PPC ad campaigns yield significant information about visitors who arrived at your website via a mouse click and website usage reports also help you identify which parts of your website are reaching their goals and which are not (tracked by the number and behavior of visitors who visited those pages). If the website works and converts well using PPC, it is likely that it will work well on other online advertising media.

- ◆ PPC ads can easily and quickly be changed to take visitors to different landing pages, or customized to bring some visitors to one landing page and others to another version for comparative purposes. This allows you to improve your site's conversion process more quickly than SEO on its own.

- ◆ Likewise, PPC ad links can quickly be changed to promote a seasonal or other special marketing initiative, leading visitors via the landing page to details of the promotion. For example, if your company plans a marketing promotion for Valentine's Day, the ad can quickly be tailored to reflect this and the landing page altered, if necessary.

- ◆ Pay per click is also a good option to try if your website isn't getting the amount or type of traffic expected. Additional SEO may help, but a PPC ad will immediately encourage visitors to click and visit your website. Analysis of that traffic can help you make changes that can alter the quality and quantity of visitors you receive much more quickly.

Keep in mind that with PPC advertising, you do not have to wait months to see the results of your effort, as you do with regular search engine optimization. Some PPC search engines do take a few days to have an editor check over submitted ads for relevance, and to ensure they do not violate the search engine's terms of service. However, realizing that timing is one of the major advantages of PPC advertising, most PPC providers get your ad up and running as soon as possible.

This can be particularly beneficial for companies that have just opened for business, because it gives them an opportunity to compete online almost instantaneously.

Why Is Pay-Per-Click Advertising So Effective?

Now that we've explored how pay per click can help augment your search engine optimization program, let's look at why it is such an effective method, both to searchers and in comparison to other forms of online advertising.

Besides the fact that the location of PPC ads on results pages is usually in the viewing area that draws a visitor's eye more quickly than other parts of the page, the actual ad component itself has many advantages over other types of online advertising that result in its overall lead in effectiveness.

The key to this effectiveness is how the searcher views this form of advertising and their acceptance of it, in comparison to their relatively weaker response to other types of online advertising, such as banner ads or popup ads. In part, this is because PPC ads remain a relative novelty compared to banner and popup ads, which have been highly visible on websites for many years.

Searchers find great utility in PPC ads, mainly because they are clear in what they are selling. General search results may or may not lead to companies actually selling products, but because these ads are paid advertising, it's completely logical to searchers that when they click on such an ad, they will go to a website with relevant products or services.

In effect, the audience is already targeted and pre-qualified—your PPC ad will be clicked on by people already interested in your product, resulting in better conversion rates than organic search listings.

Other types of online advertising do not deliver to the advertiser the same kinds of benefits a pay-per-click ad does. Some of the reasons why PPC ads are more popular among advertisers than other types of online marketing include:

- ♦ PPC ads can be crafted so as to include your most important keywords and unique information that will lead a user to click, even though they are much smaller in size than banner or skyscraper-style ads.

- ♦ PPC ads are text-only (except for the occasional search engine that allows the addition of a logo in the ad). Research has proven that text ads have more influence on searchers because they provide information to help them make a decision, rather than flashy graphics with little detail.

- ♦ Whether people are looking to buy products online, or are just researching products they will later buy locally, they have little time to waste. They prefer ads that tell them as much as possible about the website and its products so they don't waste time investigating sites that don't fit their needs.

- ♦ PPC ads found on search engine results pages reach a larger potential audience than banner or popup ads placed on a website or in an online news source. Research shows that up to 80% of people who are online use either Google and/or Yahoo! Those people are exposed to PPC ads on a regular basis. Even if the searcher doesn't click on your ad, you may have made an impression on their mind at no cost to you.

They may remember your company's name later when they are looking for whatever it is that you sell. They may not have been at the "ready to buy" step when they made their first search.

◆ Other forms of online advertising tend to be much more expensive than PPC ads. This is due, in part, to the fact that no payment is due until someone clicks on the PPC ad. Other forms of advertising show up on the page regardless of whether or not the viewer is looking for the product you are advertising.

◆ It is relatively simple for an advertiser to calculate the return on investment (ROI) of a PPC ad campaign because the advertiser is only charged when someone clicks on the ad. Statistics on how many clicks were made during a certain time period, and an enormous amount of analysis of visitors' behavior while on your website (such as which pages they visited, how long they stayed, and so on) are easily captured.

The advertiser knows the cost of the ad campaign, because they control the cost via bidding on keywords, and can track how many searchers were converted into buyers. This makes figuring out whether the PPC ad was profitable or not a relatively simple calculation.

As an example, let's assume that during the month of January your PPC ad cost you $50 in clicks and that you made net sales of $100 that you can tie directly to that PPC ad. The ad was clearly successful—you earned $50 from it that month.

With an online banner ad as a contrasting example, payment is usually based on a CPM basis, or a specific cost per every thousand impressions or views of the page containing the ad. With a cost-per-impression type ad, you cannot even be certain that the searcher saw your ad on the page, just that they visited the page. Even if they ignored your ad completely, you still have to pay for it.

The cost of banner ads varies, depending on the popularity of the site they are appearing on, and average anywhere from $5 to $50 per 1000 page views. You will owe this amount, regardless of how many people actually see your ad. In addition, over the past few years, banners have continued to lose effectiveness, as users simply have come to ignore them.

Another aspect where PPC ads dominate against other methods of online advertising is the ease of changing the display and content of that ad. The text of PPC ads can be quickly changed and search engine's editors (who must review and approve text changes to ads) are usually quick to oblige. Changing the text or a graphic on other types of online advertising can be a lot more complicated and time-consuming.

To summarize, pay-per-click advertising is considered more effective by a growing number of online advertisers, for a number of very valid reasons. Basically, two things are vital. Advertisers know that searchers have been pre-qualified as interested in the product, and advertisers know they are only charged when someone clicks on the ad.

Do Different Businesses Benefit From Different Aspects of PPC?

Although almost any business can benefit from pay-per-click online advertising campaigns, some aspects of the model are of more utility to some types of businesses than to others.

First, many PPC search engines offer exposure to international markets; some even offer country-specific versions of their search engines. Thus, your PPC ad can appear in, for example, the United Kingdom and France, if you wish to cover those markets as well. If you are looking for international sales, these types of ads give you the flexibility you need to reach your target market(s).

Second, there are varying levels of "hands on" involvement required of the advertiser in the entire process. For example, if you are a novice, most search engines offer free assistance of some sort, although free advice is usually limited in scope. Other search engines offer a "self-serve" option, where you do all the work of setting up the advertising campaign, or a "full-serve" option where they will help you with every step, usually for a one-time flat fee.

If you want complete control of the process and/or feel experienced enough to craft your ad campaigns yourself, most PPC providers encourage you to do so. However, they all retain some degree of editorial control over what is said in the ad, and some search engines have restrictions on the types of content they will allow you to advertise. For example, some search engines do not allow ads promoting adult or gambling (gaming) websites.

As long as your website meets some fairly general rules, you can create and manage your PPC account as closely as you wish and make all the decisions yourself. This allows you to be in complete control and better informed about all the details of the ROI on the ad.

Still, advertisers need to realize that this level of control also means investing a fair amount of time to micromanage the ad campaign. This is especially true if you do not want to take advantage of any of the account management tools, such as auto bidding, that are increasingly a part of today's pay-per-click advertising products. As search engines continue to compete for advertisers, these types of tools will increase in number and sophistication.

There are also many third-party tools available that can help you manage and control your ad campaigns if you wish to receive assistance from an independent business. Some of these tools will be discussed and reviewed in detail later in this book, but basically they can help with keyword choices, bid management, visitor monitoring, and keeping track of ROI and other metrics.

For those businesses that feel they need "unbiased" information, not just the reports and information provided by the search engines, these tools can be very useful as a backup to personal monitoring of the results of your ad campaigns.

Still, some personal involvement is strongly recommended so you are familiar with all of the terminology and types of information that is included in reports from both the search engine and any third-party tool or service you have chosen.

Some advertisers are reluctant to experiment with pay-per-click ads because they believe that they work better for some types of businesses than others. However, this is not accurate. Although it is probably easier to succeed with this type of advertising if one is selling certain types of products or services, this is more a reflection of consumer preferences than the viability of pay per click itself. For instance, it is unlikely that consumers will ever purchase a house from an online ad without conducting some other kind of research. However, they will routinely purchase lower-cost, or more frequently purchased, items as a result of any kind of online advertising.

What pay per click offers you as a distinct advantage over other types of online advertising is its **immediacy of placement** and **flexibility** in making changes.

Another stumbling block for pay-per-click advertising in the past was that businesses with a strictly local market were reluctant to place such ads, because they feared ROI would be low to nonexistent. Their reasoning was that unless their products were those that searchers have historically shown a propensity to purchase online (such as books, music, and DVDs), they would be charged for the clicks, but receive few conversions from visitors into buyers—unless those visitors were from the same general locale as the business.

Search engines aware of this dilemma began to offer versions of "local search" to their engines. Once the giants in the search industry (and huge providers of PPC advertising), Google and Yahoo! released their local search programs early in 2004, advertisers became interested in locally targeted paid advertising.

Because the lure of targeting a local audience was too great to resist, many of the other PPC search engines have developed local search capabilities, in part to keep their niche market advertisers from migrating to larger search engines.

Although just recently released from beta mode, advertisers are investigating Google AdWords Local Search, where you enter not only a keyword or phrase, but also a city or zip code. The search then returns organic search results for that specific area, together with geographically targeted pay-per-click ads, as well as links to maps and other local information.

We'll cover the topic of local search in much more detail later in this book. We will also provide information on the options offered by various search engines.

Research Results Show the Growing Importance of Pay Per Click

A number of research studies conducted throughout 2004 show that the trend toward pay-per-click advertising is increasing, as is the use of the Internet by consumers for purchasing products or services.

Results of a study conducted by The Kelsey Group and BizRate.com, posted in February of 2004, suggest that up to 25% of all searches by online buyers are local in nature, and close to 40% of all search activity is related to shopping.

The study group consisted of a statistically significant group of web searchers who had purchased something online in the past year. 64% of this group also indicated that search engines were the "main way" they accessed something online, and almost half (44%) reported conducting more local search queries for businesses than they had in the previous year.

A study by Pew/Internet published in January 2005, showed that almost two-thirds (62%) of those using the Internet still don't understand there are two different types of listings on a search engine results page—non-paid (organic) and paid.

This study is particularly interesting because they took the remaining 38% of users (who were aware of paid advertising on search results pages) and asked them some follow-up questions. Of those who said they've previously used search engines with paid results, over half (54%) have clicked on a pay-per-click ad.

About 70% of respondents approve of paid advertising because it means the search engines can remain free of cost to users. 21% said they did not like paid advertising mixed in, and would pay extra for a non-ad-based search engine.

Another interesting finding is that if it were made perfectly clear that a search engine was tracking an individual's searches in order to personalize upcoming ads, just over one-fifth (21%) of all Internet searchers would stop using that search engine.

As Deborah Fellows, the author of the survey report wrote, this state of affairs places a large burden on search engines to maintain confidence and trust by ensuring the perception of unbiased, fair search results. This will continue to become increasingly more difficult as the presence of paid advertising in search results becomes more and more obvious.

Is Pay Per Click Replacing Other Methods of Online Advertising?

The growing popularity of PPC advertising through the last couple of years has led to many changes in online methods of advertising.

Most significant of all, the rapid growth of PPC ads in combination with local search was an impetus to a process already underway—the gradual migration of advertisers from print to online yellow and white pages, either in place of traditional print advertising, or in addition to continuing print advertising.

Pay per click is definitely making in a dent in other types of online advertising. Its ease of use, relatively low cost, quick setup or shutdown, ease of making changes to ad campaigns, as well as detailed tracking and management options available, have led many online advertisers using other methods to turn to PPC.

Because it costs relatively little to experiment with PPC, many smaller advertisers will give it a try and then compare the results to other, more traditional, methods such as banner ads or popup ads. The addition of local search has businesses even more intrigued, given that research from The Kelsey Group has shown that over 60% of all search engine traffic is somehow locally related, and that by the year 2008 the market for local search advertising is estimated to be $2.5 billion.

A WebInternet survey also showed that 59% of respondents would use pay-per-click advertising if they could target a specific location, an option that is now becoming commonplace in search engines.

Although other methods of online and offline advertising have strengths and advantages over pay-per-click ads, the significant advantages of **quick results** and **the ability to self-manage your ad campaign, now enhanced with the option of targeting a local market**, makes it very likely that the trend will not just continue, but increase. As further enhancements become available, PPC advertising will become even more desirable, both for advertisers and the visitors/buyers they are seeking.

Searchers have made it abundantly clear, both via their responses to market research and in their actions, that they are tired of popup advertising interfering with their search experience. Many are increasingly using "popup blocker" applications. Banner advertising is becoming less popular as well. Unless the banner itself is very compelling in design, The Kelsey Group's research finds that viewers may glance at the top headline or heading, but rarely will look further at a banner ad. There are many reasons for this, but the main one is that, when asked, online buyers rank text-based ads much higher than graphic ads with very little text, the category most banner ads fit into.

Conclusion

What has happened in the search engine marketing arena over the last couple of years is a fundamental shift from traditional means of online advertising to a previously little-used option called pay-per-click advertising.

Because PPC has plenty of advantages, and few disadvantages, many more companies are starting to begin experimenting with this type of advertising.

As companies continue to experience the benefits of PPC ads (such as having an easier way to compute the ROI on ad campaigns), search engines and companies with third-party support tools react with enhancements or new features that help advertisers with the nuts and bolts of creating and managing a PPC ad campaign.

The end result will be the continued growth of the PPC advertising model over the next few years. Other forms of paid online advertising are adjusting their approach in response to the success of PPC and to what research is now telling us about people who visit search engines for shopping purposes.

For now, however, pay-per-click advertising is quite possibly the most cost-effective and efficient means of online advertising available, with improvements to the process being made almost daily by one search engine or another. Small-to-medium-sized businesses can no longer afford to "wait and see" before trying this type of advertising—the introduction of localized search to the mix is the final factor that should sway you to consider investigating this form of advertising.

In the following chapter, we will discuss how to set up a pay-per-click advertising campaign, from choosing a search engine and writing your initial ad to tracking the results. In the process, we will also show you how powerful this form of advertising can be.

Chapter 4 – Developing a Successful Ad Campaign

So far, we have discussed the concept of pay-per-click advertising, how it differs from search engine optimization and other advertising techniques, and the results that this type of advertising can bring to businesses.

Now it is time to delve into the nuts-and-bolts portion of this book. Because you've read this far, you are undoubtedly interested in experimenting with PPC to see if it can improve the performance of your online advertising campaigns, in terms of producing more sales without incurring higher costs than you are already paying for other sales methods. Using the tips and techniques described in this chapter, along with a couple of hours of your time and about a hundred dollars, you will be able to set up ad campaigns on several search engines and then evaluate their effectiveness.

> Most search engines require a minimum deposit between $25 and $50, which usually goes completely toward your first clicks.

As you read through this chapter, keep the following points in mind, especially when you are ready to open an advertiser account.

- ◆ **Choose your search engine(s) wisely.** Search engines differ in the type of pay-per-click services they offer and in the audience they appeal to and serve. Consequently, the same ad on different search engines will have different results.

- ◆ **An ad written for this type of advertising is very different in nature from other forms of marketing.** Certain aspects of your products or services should be prominent in PPC ads, although you may consider them secondary in other forms of advertising.

- ◆ **Re-think the way you write ads.** Search engines restrict not just the length of your message, but also stop you from using terms that you may consider vital to attracting potential buyers, such as "the greatest bargain online" and similar superlatives, unless you can prove your claim on the page you direct visitors to. Despite this, you still need to find a unique selling point that will attract the eye of someone browsing the search results page.

- ◆ **You must entice visitors to click on your ad.** Without a carefully crafted ad, you will not profit from your undertaking, even if you have paid for the privilege of having your ad appear at the top of the PPC listings (you have successfully bid for that position).

♦ **The ultimate purpose is to attract <u>quality</u> visitors.** Because you pay each time someone clicks on your ad, your success is measured by actual sales or by visitors taking other actions that you have decided are part of your ad campaign goal (such as signing up for your newsletter). The more specific the ad is, the more targeted the visitor will be, and the higher the number of conversions you will receive.

Opening an Advertiser Account on a PPC Search Engine

Opening an advertiser account with any pay-per-click search engine is usually simple and fairly intuitive. Generally speaking, all you need is a list of the keywords or phrases you wish to use, the final copy for your ad, and the URL of the landing page you wish to send visitors to. Many search engines even have a wizard that will guide you step-by-step through the process, often with interactive help if you have questions along the way.

However, the opening of the account is actually the easy part. Before you do open an account, much preparation is required. Plus, once you have opened an account you will need to tweak your ad campaign(s) as frequently as possible to ensure you are receiving the best results possible and generating a positive return on investment. For this aspect, you may use a combination of the information provided by the search engine to its advertisers, third-party tools and services related to pay-per-click advertising, and your own observations of the direction of your results.

Let's begin with a discussion of some of the factors you need to consider when writing your ad for inclusion in a PPC advertising program.

Writing a PPC Ad That Generates Results

Your ultimate goal is to write a pay-per-click ad that will strike the optimal balance between receiving the largest amount of targeted traffic and making the most conversions, in terms of sales and leads.

The ad itself generally consists of several parts—the title of the ad, a description, and the visible URL of the page you want to send visitors to. Most search engines have fairly strict parameters concerning the length and appearance of text allowed in the title and description portions of the ad. Yahoo! Search Marketing ads, for example, consist of three basic parts:

♦ **Title or Headline**—this section of your ad is limited to a maximum of 40 characters. It is highly recommended that you use the keyword you are basing your pay-per-click ad on in the title, for two very important reasons. First, if the searcher's keyword is also in your title, he or she will perceive your ad to be more targeted toward their specific needs.

Second, many search engines bold the keyword when it appears in the title/headline or the description of your ad, thus attracting more attention to it. We will discuss keyword and bidding techniques later.

- **Description**—this part of the ad is limited to 190 characters (other search engines allow anywhere from 100 to 250 characters). The description should succinctly state the unique selling point you wish to use to catch a searcher's eye—the benefit or feature of your product that will entice the searcher to click on your ad rather than your competitors' ads. Be as specific as possible. Concentrate more on describing your product than using sales talk or superlatives that do not describe what you are offering. Focus on action words and avoid using the term "free" (even if you have a free offer on your website); you will receive huge numbers of clicks from searchers curious about anything that is identified as "free," and those visitors don't tend to convert well.

- **URL**—this is the landing page to which your visitors will be redirected once they click on your ad. This field allows 1024 characters, to enable you to designate a page deep within your site as the desired landing page if you choose to do so. We will discuss how to choose and/or design a good landing page in an upcoming section of this chapter.

Most search engines offering PPC advertising follow similar guidelines for ad structure. Many have a lot of rules about each part of your ad—not just their length, but also about their content.

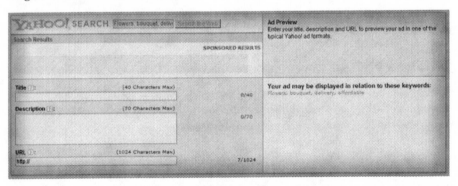

Figure 4.1 - The interface for creating a Yahoo! ad.

Some of the more restrictive rules include:

- Superlatives, such as "the best" or "top-rated" should be avoided. If you do include a superlative, ensure the content on your landing page specifically backs up that claim with a description of why you are entitled to make that claim (and still be prepared for a request to remove the term no matter how persuasive your claim is).

♦ If you are targeting a local area, both Yahoo! and Google strongly suggest that you work the name of the city, region, or state into the ad.

♦ If the text of your ad mentions a special deal or promotion, full details should be within 1-2 clicks of your landing page.

Other search engines, especially smaller, second-tier search engines, may be a little more flexible in terms of editorial guidelines, but few provide the amount of online guidance concerning acceptable ad characteristics offered by Google and Yahoo! Instead, most just state that your submitted PPC ad is subject to review and changes by their editors before being placed on the search engine.

While designing your ad, take time to investigate your competition. Find out who the main players in your industry are and look at a number of their PPC ads to get an idea of the kind of phrasing they are using. This approach can help you whether you are new to the process or a seasoned advertiser struggling to come up with compelling verbiage. Your competitors' ads may provide just the inspiration you need to create an ad even more attractive than theirs.

Because the content of your ad can be changed as often as you wish, constantly test and retest your ads. Remember that there isn't a single point in time when you will come up with the perfect campaign, and you can say "I'm done." No matter how well your ads are performing, you must always experiment and try to improve your results, or you risk being overtaken by your competition.

As a final note, because PPC ads are dynamic and can be changed quickly, you can also use them to highlight a special promotion or a special feature of your product or service that sets you apart from the competition.

If you choose to do this, be certain the landing page for the PPC ad has all the information the visitor needs about that special promotion or feature.

Most PPC search engines offer help with crafting your PPC ad at little or no charge. Others will take over the entire process for a somewhat higher price—the attraction being that they have the expertise and experience to know what works and what doesn't in a PPC ad.

Google AdWords offers a service called "JumpStart" where they set up the entire campaign for you for $299 (you are required to commit to a minimum $50 daily budget). The entire payment will be applied toward your clicks. Yahoo! offers a similar service called FastTrack® at a cost of $199. However, the payment is not applied to your account at Yahoo! Other search engines offer similar services in the $99-$150 range.

Of course, keep in mind that when you pay somebody to design your campaign, its success depends entirely on a stranger's perception of the unique qualities of your particular product or service, and how much time they are allotted by the search engine for each customer.

Some business owners prefer to have complete control over the content of the ad from start to finish, while others are content to leave all the decisions in the hands of the search engine's employees.

We recommend that you set up the campaign yourself if at all possible, but contact your account executive at the search engine(s) for advice and tips on how to improve your pay-per-click ad's content and which additional features may help you get the most for your click charges. Remember, it is also in any search engine's best interests that you succeed as an advertiser.

If you are new to the PPC ad game, take advantage of every opportunity for help, especially if it does not add to your advertising costs. You have nothing to lose, and at worst, you will come away from the experience with more knowledge than you had before about which action words you should use and what types of phrases fail to motivate viewers.

Also, try out all the free tools, such as those that suggest keywords and provide their current costs. If free editorial advice is offered, and you have the time to confer with your account executive about your ad, always take advantage of this option. After all, the search engines PPC consultants have been at this game longer than you have. You should take advantage of their knowledge, especially if it is included as a free service.

Whatever level of expertise you have with PPC ads, it is important that you test and experiment with different descriptions and titles, track the results over a set time period, and then compare them to one another. Use testing to:

♦ Ascertain which combination of description and/or title works best for attracting visitors to click your ad and visit your website.

♦ Determine ways to encourage visitors to follow the logical progression you have set up on your website to convince them of the utility of your product/service.

♦ Find effective means of converting him/her into a buyer (and hopefully, a repeat purchaser).

Choosing Keywords That Work Best for Your Business

Keywords for a pay-per-click ad play a vital role—convincing users to enter your website to enable you to persuade them to purchase the products and services you sell.

As an advertiser, you bid on keywords that describe your business, product, or service. This allows you to secure a ranking within the PPC ad section on the results page for that keyword when a user types it into the search box on the search engine. Thus, careful keyword selection is essential to attract qualified (or interested) prospects.

The first step in creating a list of keywords for a PPC ad campaign is to sit down, open a Notepad file, and simply start brainstorming about the terms you think people may use to search when looking for whatever it is that you are selling.

> Because general keywords (such as "travel") tend to be highly sought after, competitive and costly, it makes sense to develop keyword variations to secure low-cost bids.

Keep in mind that the more keywords you have, the more traffic and conversions you'll be likely to attract.

It is almost always best to choose keywords that are specific to your business rather than to include very general keywords.

Remember that the goal is not to simply attract visitors, but to attract prospects interested in what you are selling.

Otherwise, you may end up paying for clicks from people who are looking for specific products or services that you do not offer.

For example, if you were a local shop selling notebook computers, you may not want to bid on the keyword "computers" because this could attract people looking for computer service, personal computers, computer advice, and many other things that have nothing to do with the notebook computers you sell.

Furthermore, the cost of general keywords is usually quite high. For example, on Yahoo!, the number-one position for the word "computers" is $3.48 per click, while "notebook computers" costs $2.68 cents per click.

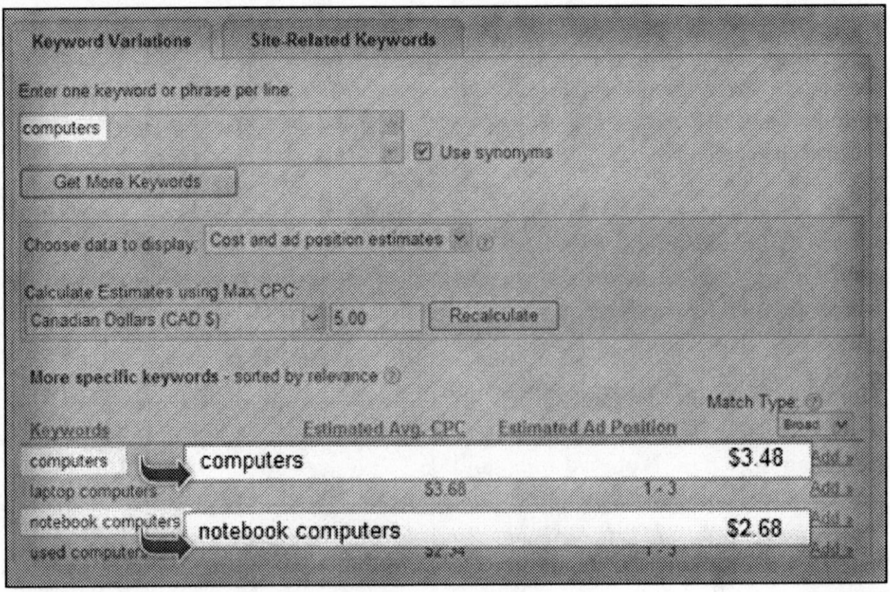

Figure 4.2 – The first position for a general term, such as "computers" on Yahoo! is $3.48, while a more specific one, "notebook computers," is just $2.68.

In other words, by selecting more specific keywords, you attract higher-quality prospects at a lower cost. Of course, keep in mind that cheaper keywords tend to get less traffic than general ones, but you can make up for that by creating a large number of keywords.

Search engines offer a lot of control over the parameters of your advertising campaign, especially as far as keywords are concerned. Many also offer you the opportunity to set the level or degree to which your keywords match a visitor's search query. Using this technique, you can influence the degree of targeting to find the best balance of general and specific keywords for your business.

Common misspellings (such as "ocassion" instead of "occasion") or other variations on your keyword (e.g., inoffensive slang, acronyms, or a shortened version of the word that is commonly used) may cost a great deal less than your regular keywords, but still have a great deal of utility. Keep in mind that major search engines have begun automatically correcting spelling mistakes in the search box, which may erode the value of adding low-cost, commonly misspelled keywords to your advertising plans.

Some search engines provide very useful keyword suggestion tools. The advertiser enters potential keywords and the tool suggests related terms and provides the monthly search volume for each. One of the most popular of these tools is the Keyword Selector Tool located at Yahoo! See Appendix 3 for details.

Keyword Selection Tools

Many tools are available to help quickly and easily generate keywords—some provided by search engines and others from independent companies.

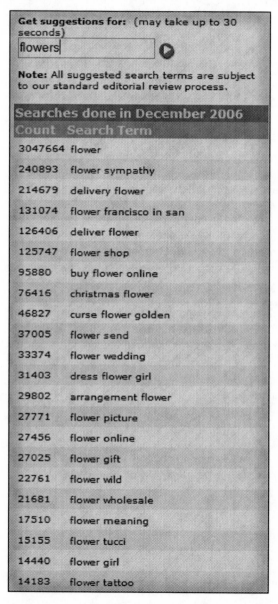

The most popular of the third-party tools is located at WordTracker.com. This tool shows up to 1,000 keywords and keyword combinations similar to those you enter, along with how many competing pages exist for that word/phrase and how frequently the keywords have been searched for.

The WordTracker database contains over 300 million searches collected over the previous 90 days.

Armed with this information, you can experiment with different keywords on the search engine to see the cost per click of different keyword variations to ensure they fit into your budget and are a good fit for your products/services.

Many advertisers still use the Yahoo! keyword search tool, which is so popular that it is at times difficult to connect to, due to such high demands on it. There are many other free tools available, some of which are identified later in this book in Appendix 3, Recommended Resources.

Figure 4.3 – Yahoo! will generate keyword variations and show the number of searches for each during the previous month.

There is one major consideration to keep in mind when working with the keyword-generating tools found on major search engines like Google and Yahoo! and third-party tools. If you run tests of the major search engine tools and WordTracker or another niche engine keyword tool, you will undoubtedly be presented with totally different keyword lists and search volume figures.

This reinforces our position that selecting the most appropriate keywords for your PPC ad requires looking at more than one keyword generation tool. If your time is limited, look at one search engine tool and one third-party product (at the minimum) to improve your chances of making the best choices for your situation.

Virtually the same argument is true when you talk about tracking keyword performance. The next chapter of this book covers tracking every aspect of your PPC ad. For now, let's just say that the rule of using a backup tracking system in the form of a third-party product is always a good idea.

The reports you receive from any search engine are sometimes put together using certain assumptions, and the use of a third-party product to double-check your results can highlight discrepancies in keyword performance. You then can discuss these discrepancies with your account representatives to discover reasons behind differences.

When it comes to deciding which keywords to use, we cannot stress enough the importance of experimentation. Even with a relatively small ad campaign budget, you can still run week-long campaigns using different keywords on different search engines and see what works best for you. The more combinations of search engines and keywords you try, the more effective, and less costly, your ad campaign will ultimately be.

Keyword Matching Options

Let's use the Google keyword matching options program as an example of how best to target keywords. Other search engines offer comparable setups.

Google offers three basic choices:

- ◆ Broad Match
- ◆ Phrase Match
- ◆ Exact Match

The default is **Broad Match**, which means that if your business only sells microwave ovens and you choose this two-word combination as a keyword, your ad may appear on results pages where users entered either the word "microwave" or the word "ovens."

If you are selling a fairly common item, not only may the keyword cost be high for such a match, but the results will be much less targeted than you would like and you may wind up with a lot of non-converting clicks on your ad.

A much more productive option in the Google model is to use **Phrase Match** and/or **Exact Match**. For Phrase Match, put quotation marks around your keywords as you enter them when setting up your account. Your ad will then only be shown when a searcher uses the entire phrase in that specific word order, although you still may be shown on results pages for search terms that contain words in addition to "microwave ovens," such as those specifying a particular wattage or color.

However, ads dealing only with microwave–related subjects will no longer appear. You will receive fewer responses from searchers, but those who see your ad will be interested specifically in microwave ovens (rather than any other kind of microwave product or type of oven).

Phrase matching more closely targets your audience and brings you results more likely to lead to conversion.

Exact Match is even more restrictive. By entering your keywords with brackets around them (e.g., [microwave ovens]) you ensure that your ad will only appear when a searcher uses that exact phrase, in that exact word order, and with no additional words in their query.

Depending upon your business, and the number of words you include in the phrase, Exact Match can be so restrictive that you will show up very infrequently on results pages.

> Negative keywords are a useful way to limit searches, but should be utilized with caution to ensure you don't limit your ad's appearance by too many restricting factors.

Let's presume that you only sell microwave ovens that are blue in color. If you use Exact Match with the phrase [blue microwave ovens], you are likely to receive far fewer clicks because you have targeted your market so closely. However, those that you do receive are more likely to convert into buyers because they have found someone selling exactly what they want.

Another option available on most search engines is **Negative Keywords**. This option ensures that your ad will not appear if any of the words you indicate (via a preceding negative sign [-]) as negative keywords in your keyword list are included in the search phrase.

For example, if you don't sell blue microwave ovens, choosing the word "-blue" as a negative keyword will ensure that anyone typing in a search for "blue microwave ovens" will not see your ad.

Build up your list of negative keywords over time, based on the reports you receive from your search engine and/or third-party tools on keyword performance.

Controlling Your Costs

The expense of a PPC ad campaign can vary from a small investment to thousands of dollars per month. Part of the preparation of your ad is deciding how much money your company is willing to put aside for PPC ad campaigns.

If you have a fairly small budget, spend the extra time necessary to discover low-cost keywords. You may also want to investigate some of the smaller search engines, whose prices may be more in line with your budget.

The smaller engines do not get the same amount or quality of traffic as the larger players, but they do attract niche searchers, so can be effective if your product is one that appeals to certain markets more than others. Generally speaking, smaller search engines have lower keyword costs, so that even with less traffic they have the potential to provide a higher conversion rate to advertisers.

Bidding for Keywords

Once you have come up with a list of keywords and decided which search engine(s) you are going to run your PPC ad campaign on, start bidding for keywords.

The concept of bidding is fairly simple. The more you pay, the higher in the paid advertising results section your ad will appear.

Most major search engines have implemented minimum bid requirements for PPC ads, ranging from 3 cents to 10 cents.

On occasion, search engines increase the minimum price of keyword bids. For example, at one point Yahoo! Search Marketing raised the minimum cost per click from 5 cents to 10 cents. Bids in the 5 to 9 cent range were "grandfathered" in and allowed to continue at those levels as long as the advertiser wished.

However, it wasn't long before bidding on a number of keywords went to 10 cents or over, because as soon as a new advertiser opened an account with your keyword(s), they immediately outbid keywords in the 5-9 cent range since they had to submit a 10-cent minimum bid.

Google changed the keyword bidding paradigm in mid-2005 when they introduced the "Quality Score" concept, where minimum bid amounts for keywords are based on an estimate by Google of how "relevant" your ad is for that keyword. It set off a storm of protest when Google added the "quality" of your landing page into the mix as well. We'll look at the Quality Score issue in more detail later.

Manual Bidding Versus Auto-Bidding

With bidding, you can either handle the process manually or let a search engine auto bid for you, using settings you have chosen. For example, on Yahoo! Search Marketing, the auto-bid feature allows you to do one of two things: you can either "bid to position" where your maximum bid will automatically be changed to be set at 1 cent above any competing bids, in order to maintain your selected position, or you can set one maximum bid for all of the keywords you select from among your list.

The advantages of auto bidding are relatively self-explanatory. Auto bidding allows you to control your PPC campaign costs without having to be involved personally. The search engine will automatically adjust your keyword bids according to the parameters you have set, thus controlling the amount of money you spend; this frees you from having to monitor and then change keyword bids.

The major disadvantage to automatic bidding is precisely that—it is "automatic." Even though you may have set certain conditions on changing bids (such as a maximum bid for a certain keyword to retain a rank of second), and some search engines and third-party tools have complex auto-bidding functions called rules-based bidding, automatic bidding techniques have still not been perfected. An auto-bidding program may miss opportunities that manual observation by the advertiser may have noticed.

Relying totally on auto bidding can have another downside as well. A competitor may begin bidding against you in such a way as to discover your maximum bid by instigating a "bidding war" until your search engine reaches your maximum bid.

Your competitor then can either set their bid to be just one cent above you, or, if they have a lot of money and really want to dominate that keyword, they can bid you to maximum and just wait until your budget runs out.

However, if you had been present when someone was trying to do such a thing, you would have noticed the pattern of a "bid war" and perhaps abandoned the "war" before your budget was completely gone, and instead switched to a lower page rank. By watching the bidding yourself (even with the aid of tools), you can manipulate the bidding so as to get the highest page rank for specific keywords in a more fine-tuned manner; you are actively making decisions, not just relying on some general bidding rules being applied, as happens with auto bidding.

The subject of auto bidding almost naturally leads us to the next consideration in your ad campaign—the position of your ad in the PPC listings.

Ad Positioning

The number of available positions varies depending upon the search engine, and even upon the resolution of the searcher's computer screen at times, but it is generally limited to five to eight ads.

The top three listings are the ones with the highest amount of traffic. For one thing, these top three listings are more likely to wind up in the **syndicated listings** (that is, those that are shown on partner sites, so you get extended reach of your ad without additional payments).

However, the interesting aspect of this is that the higher you are listed, the fewer conversions to sales/actions you are likely to have.

As you move down in the positions, the conversions of clicks to sales/actions will increase and the bid prices will decrease. However, the overall amount of traffic will go down.

> Generally, the best positions to occupy are between 2 and 5. Position number 1 will deliver the highest amount of traffic, but the lowest conversions.

Your goal is to find the golden middle. If your ad appears too low in the listings, your traffic will vanish. However, occupy the first position and you'll wind up paying for a lot of wasted clicks. Although this may vary from industry to industry, we have found that positions two to five tend to be the most effective.

Positions two to five may be more effective for a PPC ad campaign because people often click on the first listing out of curiosity, rather than true interest or intent to purchase.

Therefore, the top-ranked position in PPC ad listings often receive a number of clicks that don't necessarily come from someone already interested in the product and ready to purchase it.

By being in the second or third position, you will receive clicks from visitors requiring more information than they received at the first website or those looking for comparisons on features and pricing between your site and the others.

A visitor may click on the first ad, find out all they need to know about the product and its price there, and then click on the second ad to comparison shop. They may or may not then move on to the third ad, or go somewhere else for further comparison shopping, if they are truly interested in purchasing.

Some people are just interested in what type of websites might be advertising such items and others may just be beginning the buying cycle and using the first ad as a place to begin their research on features of the product, cost, availability, etc.

However, if the price of the product is roughly the same between the first advertiser and this second one, the visitor will often purchase the product right then, on the second-listed PPC ad site, rather than going back to the first site.

If the visitor does return to the first site to purchase, the profit margin on that sale is slightly less than it could have been, because the conversion of this visitor into a buyer took two clicks rather than one, so the advertiser has to pay for two clicks at whatever price the keyword is currently bidding at. For many products this may be a matter of just a few cents, but this can be costly if your keywords cost dollars for each click.

Another factor to consider is the expected screen resolution of the average user. Ads that are positioned "above the fold" usually perform better than those appearing below this point, since they do not require scrolling to see them. Different screen resolutions will yield different points where the "fold" falls. Experiment with some search engines at different screen resolutions to judge where the "fold" appears and keep this in mind when bidding to position.

Bid Gaps

Another vital aspect to understand with keyword bidding is the problem of **bid gaps**. Bid gaps occur when you have established a keyword price you are willing to pay based on the situation at the time the campaign was set up, and then a change occurs as a result of a bidding war or other circumstance that results in your ad remaining in place while the bid just below yours is much lower.

Bid gaps happen most frequently when you are not monitoring your ad campaign closely enough. Some search engines will automatically close bid gaps for you and third-party tools are also available to screen for bid gaps, but you also should keep an eye out for them each time you review your ad campaigns.

If the gap between your keyword bid and the cost for the ad listed directly beneath you is large, you are paying too much for the keyword and your ad budget may decline alarmingly before you realize what has occurred.

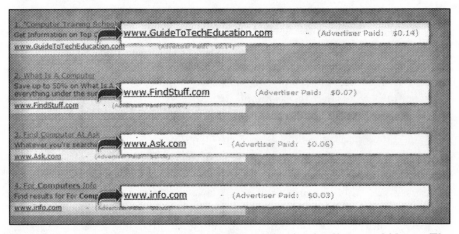

Figure 4.4 – An example of poor campaign monitoring leading to a bid gap. The first advertiser could get the same position for just 8 cents, instead of 14 cents.

Landing Pages

Once you've chosen your keywords, the next decision you must make concerns which page of your website you want visitors who click on your PPC ad to arrive at.

The first thought of most advertisers is to make this page (called the "landing page") the homepage of their website, because that seems to be the most logical place to begin exploring the website.

> Some webmasters construct special web pages for their PPC ad campaigns that do not show up if someone is simply browsing the general website. These pages are designed to improve the experience of users searching for specific products or services.

However, in almost every case, your landing page should be one that is specifically designed to convince the visitor to purchase your product. Alternatively, it can be what you consider to be the highest quality page on your site.

Your landing page should contain all the pertinent information (or clear links to that information) that a visitor needs in order to place an order for your product. It should highlight your product's best selling points, its unique selling point, how much it costs, how to purchase it, and so on. In short, it should be a page from which a person can order your product, or be just a click away from the order page.

The landing page is particularly important if you are targeting local searches. In such a case, you should concentrate on who your competitors are even more closely than when targeting general searches. To make the sale, you must have unique selling points on your landing page that make you look like a better place to buy the product than the store three streets away selling the same product.

You can offer special deals on the landing page, time-limited offers, free shipping if you purchase by a certain date—any kind of special incentive you are willing to offer to stop the visitor from leaving without being converted into a buyer. You can even have a collection of different landing pages, each customized somehow to appeal to a certain segment of your target

> Experiment with different landing pages on a regular basis to improve your campaign and your ROI.

market or to serve a specific need, such as a seasonal theme.

On a final note, we highly encourage you to test different landing pages using **A-B Split Testing** techniques. With this procedure, you choose a landing page that serves as your control and create another one where you change a few words or the layout and you send an equal amount of traffic to each page.

After waiting a couple of weeks for enough traffic to provide sufficient data, see which landing page performed best (A or B). If the control out-pulled the "challenger," leave the control and create another landing page to test with. If the "challenger" performed better than the control, then make it the new standard and repeat the cycle again.

There are tools and services on the market that will track everything for you and provide you with precise reports on every aspect of your experimentation. We will discuss these tools in the later chapters.

Budgeting for Pay-Per-Click Ad Campaigns

Budgeting for ad campaigns is an issue that has come up a number of times during this chapter. Thus far, however, recommendations have been of a general nature, such as "keep in mind your overall budget" or "reassess the budget you have to spend on PPC." At this point, we will present some specific tips for getting the most out of your advertising dollars.

You already know some ways to stay within your budget or to lower the cost of your PPC ads, such as constantly testing and improving your campaigns, keeping your bids at the most effective level, and so on.

Tip 1: Constantly evaluate which keywords work better than others and disable or delete those not performing well before they drain your budget.

Tip 2: Keep a close eye on your budget. You should have a rough idea of how much is left in your PPC account at any given time. As soon as your funds are depleted, all advertising stops—whether you know it or not. Most PPC search engines will notify you when you are close to depleting your account, but the lag time between you receiving the notice and replenishing the account can cost you sales.

Tip 3: Even if you use third-party tools to bid for you and to manage your campaigns, you must keep your own methods in place to keep track of how fast any given keyword is draining your account. You really do need to investigate your campaign statistics personally, and on a regular basis, to mitigate the danger of a quick turnaround in the marketplace.

Tip 4: If you are not keeping track of your campaign's budget properly, it could also be drained by one or more of the following:

♦ Click fraud

♦ An error made when setting up the ad

♦ An automated bidding tool is keeping your bids artificially high

Tip 5: Clever marketers have been known to manipulate the bidding in such a way that you pay more than you need to maintain the position you want. Unfortunately, there are unscrupulous people out there who will bypass the general rules governing pay per click and manipulate the underlying structure of the advertising model to their advantage.

All of the above tips talk about an advertiser's personal involvement in ad campaigns in one way or another. This leads to the consideration of whether outside firms are a good choice for managing your ad campaigns, if you would rather not put forth the time and effort to handle it yourself. The answer is different for each advertiser and each product, their location, the online track record of the outside firms under consideration, together with the general online advertising marketplace at the time. Basically, the answer comes down to a consideration of what makes most economic sense in your particular situation.

If nobody in your company really understands the PPC market or has the time to take care of your ad campaigns (at a minimum keeping an active eye on the automated tools), you should consider outsourcing your PPC ad campaigns. To protect your interests, choose a firm that you have thoroughly investigated and that you are sure sees the long-term goals of your PPC program in the same light as you do.

Unfortunately, the typical ad budget of small to-medium-sized companies does not stretch enough to include management of online advertising by an outside advertising firm. As a rule, firms charge up to 20% of your monthly spending and have a minimum fee of $300-$500 per month. In this is beyond your budget, you will likely need to recruit your web people to work with marketing to create, maintain, and decide when to end a particular PPC ad campaign.

Even if you can afford an outside firm, the nature of PPC ads is such that personal involvement by someone who knows the company inside and out and who has a stake in ensuring that the ads perform well, is the best road to take. PPC advertising is not as complicated to understand as it may first appear, and most people can quickly learn how to tell if a PPC ad campaign is progressing as it should, or if certain areas need to be changed or removed altogether.

> Deciding on whether or not you'd be better off managing your PPC campaigns yourself or outsourcing them to professionals depends largely on your budget and the time you can afford to invest in it.

The key component to getting the most out of your pay-per-click advertising budget, however large or small, is tracking, which is the subject of our next chapter.

Chapter 5 – Tracking Ad Campaigns

Once your pay-per-click ad campaigns are up and running, you should begin to track the results of your efforts. The primary goal of any direct-response advertising campaign is to sell a product or service or get some sort of an action from your visitor—and this type of ad campaign is no different.

You have put a lot of time, thought, and effort into crafting an ad and selecting keywords that will catch the attention of visitors and attract qualified prospects. Now you should determine whether your efforts are bearing fruit. In other words, are you converting visitors to your website into customers? To find out, you ultimately need to determine the return on your investment (ROI). This is also known as the "bottom line."

ROI is a topic that many people find intimidating, but it is really a very basic concept—ROI is the net income (sales x net per item) divided by the total campaign costs. To put it simply, ROI is a percentage that shows how much profit you have made from your advertising campaign.

The way to discover the ROI on a PPC campaign can be relatively simple or more complex, depending upon how much detail you wish to deal with and how much time you are prepared to invest. Ideally, you should track the performance of both your ad and every keyword associated with it.

Tracking your ad campaign is vital to its success. Without tracking, you will have no idea why your campaign ultimately succeeds or fails, or what is working with your campaign and what isn't.

Once you have learned the basics of ad tracking, you can tweak your campaigns, perform comparison testing, and try out some advertising ideas on a small scale before investing too much time or money on a full-fledged campaign. In effect, ad tracking will tell you how your current campaigns are performing and help you predict future behavior.

Third-Party Tracking Tools

One advantage of PPC advertising is that most elements of tracking are automatically generated for your use, and the basic interpretation of tracking results is relatively simple to understand.

If you are more experienced, you can delve as deeply as you wish and analyze every detail of your campaign. Until you feel ready to do so, tracking the most important aspects is a fairly simple operation, thanks to the myriad of tools available to help you.

Many search engines now offer varying levels of analysis of the performance of your PPC ad campaigns. For example, Google purchased Urchin (a large, well-known and respected web analytics company) in 2005 and in November of that year, integrated a version into their PPC program, Google AdWords. Google offered access to the product, dubbed "Google Analytics," at no cost to the advertiser. Subsequently, other search engines began to offer some form of web analytics integrated into their PPC programs.

Analysis of the data from your PPC ad campaigns provided to you directly from the search engine itself is useful and becomes another selling point for search engines as they compete for advertisers.

However, advertisers need to keep in mind that data analysis directly from search engines is likely to be based on, and influenced by, a search engine's internal definitions of the pieces of data used in that analysis. As useful as they may be, results will be indicative of a particular search engine's view of the data points involved.

Analytics obtained from a search engine can, and should be, the starting point for your ad-tracking efforts.

There are two other sources of relevant information and analysis that will offer a more independent viewpoint of your ad's performance—third-party ad-tracking tools and your website's log files.

Advanced users may access raw logs kept on their own server, but a great deal of experience is needed not only to track ads this way, but also to set up your dataset so that, for example, clicks made by the website owner are isolated from the rest of the data.

Which tracking method you use depends strongly upon your degree of familiarity with log files—try to integrate both methods if you are comfortable with web log files; if not, consider adding a third-party ad-tracker tool to the mix if you want to analyze all aspects of your campaign.

As Heath Clarke, the chairman and CEO of Local.com Corporation™ (formerly Interchange Corporation, the parent company of one of the largest and oldest pay-per-click search engines on the market—ePilot™, as well as developers of the highly successful search engine Local.com) said in an exclusive interview with PayPerClickUniverse.com, an informational website dealing with pay-per-click advertising.

> "Track, track, and track again. Pay-per-click advertising is direct marketing, so extensive monitoring and constant tweaking of your ad campaigns is the best way for you to get results." – Heath Clarke, Chairman and CEO of Local.com Corporation™

How Ad Trackers Work

Ad trackers are services or pieces of software that monitor all of the visitors that come to your website through your advertising campaigns. Trackers 'track' any actions visitors take on your website.

Most of these services are fairly easy to use, so even if you have limited technical skills, you can still take advantage of them and find out which of your ads is most effective.

Trackers can be especially useful if you are running comparison ads (perhaps the same ad on Google and Yahoo!) to ascertain which source is providing you with the best traffic. They also allow you to experiment with different titles, descriptions, prices, landing pages, and many other aspects of your ad.

Ad tracking tools come in one of two forms—some are actual pieces of software that you pay a flat fee for and download from a website, while others are based on a monthly fee that is often tied to the number of clickthroughs.

Two examples of good ad-tracker services are www.AdWatcher.com and www.ClickTracks.com.

What You Should Be Tracking

Although there are many aspects of your ad's performance that you should be tracking, some things are essential for you to know in order to judge whether your pay-per-click ad campaigns need changing in order to be more effective.

The main statistics you should track are:

- Number of Clicks
- Percentage of Clicks to Actions
- Number of Sales
- Total Value of Sales
- Cost of Campaign
- Total Profit
- Cost Per Click
- Cost Per Sale
- Return On Investment
- Percentages of Clicks to Sales

ID	☐	Campaign				C	A	S	Rev	Cost	Profit	CPA	CPS	CPC	ROI	C2A	C2S	A2S
+ 29	☐	HostVoice				0	0	0	$0.00	$0.00	$0.00	$0.00	$0.00	$2.00	0.0%	0.0%	0.0%	0.0%
+ 14	☐	DevTalk				0	0	0	$0.00	$0.00	$0.00	$0.00	$0.00	$0.00	0.0%	0.0%	0.0%	0.0%
+ 13	☐	Admitly				0	0	0	$0.00	$0.00	$0.00	$0.00	$0.00	$2.00	0.0%	0.0%	0.0%	0.0%
Total:						0	0	0	$0.00	$0.00	$0.00	$0.00	$0.00	$4.00	0.0%	0.0%	0.0%	0.0%

Figure 5.1 – Most tracking services gather all of this information and display it in a clear, easy-to-understand format.

Most of these terms are self-explanatory; however, percentage-based statistics are more complicated. These statistics provide you with invaluable information on the success of your ad. For example, the percentage of clicks to actions data will tell you what percent of the visitors who clicked on your ad acted (i.e., subscribed to your newsletter, visited another page within your site, or left your website immediately).

Tracking ROI

Ultimately, the most important item to track closely is known as your "Return On Investment" (usually referred to as simply ROI), which compares the total cost of your ad campaign to the profit you made from the ad, then determines a percentage which indicates how successful your ad has been.

> Net profit is the sale price of the product minus how much the product actually cost you (which includes the cost of the raw product from the manufacturer, plus things such as advertising, shipping costs, and the like).

To calculate ROI, determine your net income (the number of sales multiplied by the net income you made per sale) and divide that number by the total cost of the ad campaign.

Let's say that you sold 12 units of a particular product that has a net profit of $10. 12 x $10 equals a net income of $120. We will also assume that the total campaign costs were $100.

Therefore, the ROI is $120 divided by 100 for a 1.2 earning ratio. This translates to you having made $1.20 for each ad dollar you spent—120% ROI. In this case, you are obviously making a profit in that you are making more from the sale of the product than you are spending to purchase and market it.

> ROI figures from alternate sources analyzing the same PPC ad may differ, due to different definitions or interpretations of data from these different sources.

ROI tracking is, in most cases, fairly simple for PPC advertising. Some PPC search engines include an ROI calculation in the statistics they provide you and ad trackers may also include ROI as one of their most basic pieces of data.

Search Engine Tools and Third-Party Software

In order to track closely the previously mentioned items, you may need to use third-party software. These kinds of tools will provide you with an incredible amount of information and analysis of an individual visitor's actions from the point they click on your ad until the point they leave your website (and will even tell you where they go after they leave your site).

These tools can also track actions visitors take while on your website, such as subscribing to your online newsletter, joining your mailing list for website updates, asking for information on your affiliate program, or many other actions, including making a purchase.

All of this is very useful information that can help you decide what changes you should make to your website in order to lead visitors along the path you wish them to take.

Tracking tools like these operate by placing code on the confirmation page that comes up when a visitor purchases something or commits an action. They also place a cookie on the visitor's computer, in order to track further and future behavior and visits to your website by that unique visitor. This allows you to track repeat buyers as well.

Keep in mind that your involvement in keeping an eye on your tracking data at this stage is crucial. You need to review the reports generated in order to see what is working and what is not, and constantly challenge yourself to improve conversions.

Don't be surprised if there are differences between the PPC search engine reports and those of a third-party tool. Also, don't be surprised if your own take on things seems a little different as well.

> Expect to see a discrepancy between the PPC search engine's report and your tracking tool. A 5%-10% difference is normal and acceptable.

If you are an advanced user, you may take the raw data from your logs and perform your own analysis—the results will almost certainly differ from the other two. This does not necessarily mean that anything is wrong, or that any service is not performing correctly or adequately. If the differences are relatively small (between 5% and 10%), there is no need for great concern.

However, if you see large differences in the data provided to you, it is time to investigate further by questioning the results with your customer service representative on the PPC search engine or with the supplier of the ad-tracking tool you are using.

Let's take a quick look at the basic differences between the tracking options offered by search engines and third-party solutions.

Most search engines will provide you with only basic statistics, such as the number of clicks, the number of page views, the rate of clickthroughs, the average cost per click, and the total cost of your campaign. All major search engines do not yet offer a complete set of tracking-related statistics.

For conversion data, which is what tracking is related to, Google AdWords users can make use of the Google Conversion Tracking tool. If you decide to use this tool on your Google ad campaigns, it will track the conversion data you need by having you place a small amount of code on the page on your website where you thank a visitor for purchasing your product.

Using this tracking code, Google can then provide you with many of the relevant tracking statistics needed to make informed decisions about your ad's success.

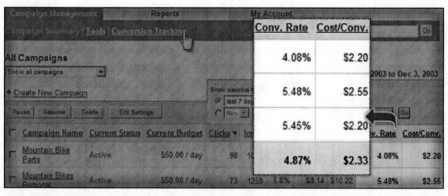

Figure 5.2 – The Google Conversion Tracking tool shows you the conversion rate and the cost for each conversion.

One disadvantage to the Conversion Tracking tool is that, by placing the tracking code on your web page, you also will see a small text box appear on that page that reads "Google Site Stats: Send Feedback," so the visitor will be aware that their activity is being tracked and analyzed and, presumably, Google can continue to amass information about the dynamics of online commerce.

Third-party tracking tools and services are numerous and tend to be much more robust than those offered by search engines, although Google and other search engines are increasingly adding features to their tracking tools to make them more competitive. In fact, Google has expanded its conversion tracking system so a user can customize it to track their ad campaigns on other search engines and report certain activities within the Google interface.

The strength of third-party tracking tools has always been their ability to show all of your various ad campaigns in an independent, comparative fashion, so that you can instantly see which search engine campaigns are most effective. Many tools now monitor click fraud, a type of computer-based fraud that has become an issue of increasing concern in the pay-per-click marketplace overall (and will be covered in detail in the next chapter).

A good example of a third-party tool that is especially useful for novices is www.AdWatcher.com, primarily because of the inclusion of excellent visual representations/demos to teach users how to use the tool most effectively. It leads you step-by-step through the process via an online setup process to take full advantage of its ability to customize almost every aspect of the tracking process and reports that are generated.

Another advantage that some third-party tools have is the ability to import your account data from Google and/or Yahoo!

There is little doubt that third-party tracking tools offer more features, but they can be relatively costly. The PPC search engine conversion tracking offered as part of your ad campaign is usually provided at no additional charge.

However, when dealing with something as important as advertising your products via pay per click, we cannot stress enough the importance of not relying on a single method of tracking. Just as you should investigate other methods of keyword bidding, you should ensure that your search engine is in sync with what other companies' products are reporting. This will require personally reviewing the reports.

Although you may not wish (or be able) to purchase the highest-priced version of a third-party tracking tool, it is certainly worth investing in one of the more basic versions. These stripped-down versions may not have all the bells and whistles, but they still do an adequate job of analyzing the visitors, actions, and sales on your website.

Some third-party tracking tools can be used for all types of online (and sometimes offline) advertising. Although we are concentrating here on their usefulness for pay-per-click advertising, they can be used for banner ads, newsletter ads, email marketing campaigns—in effect, just about any kind of advertising or marketing method used. Therefore, if you advertise in forms other than pay per click, the cost of a third-party tracking tool may be mitigated by the fact that you can use it for tracking your other ad campaigns.

The Importance of Tracking

One really can't overemphasize the importance of tracking the results of your PPC advertising campaigns. If you don't track where your visitors are going on your website, how many visitors came to your site through a particular ad campaign, how many visitors convert into buyers, your ROI, and so on, you cannot be certain if a particular ad campaign is worth continuing or not.

If you are using comparison ad campaigns to see which is most effective, the most important point to remember is to make only one change each time you run an ad test. For example, if you are testing to see which landing page works better, do not test any other aspect at the same time. If you test more than one aspect at a time, you and your tracking tools will not be able to differentiate between the two and will be unable to provide a definitive answer on which change led to more effective ad performance.

One memorable example (now a few years old but still a poignant lesson for all) is from an individual who had a PPC account with one of the major PPC search engines, paying almost $1,000 per month for all the various keywords he used. His sales revenues were quite acceptable, so he knew he was making money from his website.

Naturally, he assumed that most of the sales were coming from his ad campaign on a major search engine, because he believed that lower-cost ads placed on smaller search engines would produce lower results.

It wasn't until he became aware of ad trackers and ad tracking software that he decided to find out exactly where his sales were coming from. Using a simple ad tracker, he discovered that the vast majority of his sales were not coming from the major search engine, but instead were coming from the niche search engines, where his product had more appeal to their visitors.

He also discovered that he could drop the more expensive campaign altogether because the sales he was getting from the larger search engine equaled the amount of money he was paying for that campaign.

Without a relatively simple form of ad tracking, this individual would have continued believing that "bigger is better," and that his sales were coming from the larger search engine.

This case also emphasizes, again, the importance of using the tools that are available.

Although this incident occurred before search engines provided much data on account activity, and certainly didn't offer any form of conversion tracking, this individual may have become suspicious a lot sooner if he had investigated the statistics that were available from his search engines.

This case reiterates the importance of looking at your statistics critically and in person, not just accepting that things are proceeding as they should. Scrutiny will allow you to tweak an ad or cancel it before wasteful clicks drain your account completely.

Luckily, with both PPC search engines and third-party tracking tools

> Tracking software can help you avoid a situation such as David Ogilvy (named by Time magazine as "the most sought-after wizard in the business [of advertising]") said—"I know half of my advertising works. I just don't know which half."

competing for the market, the advertiser comes out a winner. Each side is adding more and more features, many of them free, as they compete for market share.

Click Fraud

One aspect of PPC advertising that continues to be under increasingly close investigation by both advertisers and search engines is click fraud—an unscrupulous act that can lead advertisers to abandon ad campaigns not making a profit because of fraud, rather than as a result of inherent faults in the ad or the advertiser's decisions.

Without customized tracking tools that can gather statistics about a visitor's path through your website, the increasing growth of click fraud may have gone largely unrecognized. Instead, click fraud can now be investigated and tied to specific individuals, companies, and locations.

Currently, click fraud is probably the largest single problem the industry is dealing with and, as such, deserves its own detailed discussion of the methods of click fraud and possible solutions for combating it. This is the subject of our next chapter.

Chapter 6 – Click Fraud and How to Counteract It in Ad Campaigns

Unfortunately for any advertiser or businessperson—online or offline—fraud, in one form or another, is a component with which they must deal. With offline businesses, fraud is usually in the form of shoplifting or mysteriously disappearing inventory or cash from the cash register. With online businesses, the fastest-growing type of fraud is called "click fraud."

On its most basic level, click fraud is defined as any click maliciously made on an advertiser's PPC ad with the intent of depleting the amount of money in the advertiser's account.

As a simple example, let's assume you have a pay-per-click ad set up on Google and your keyword bid is $1 per click. Therefore, each time someone clicks on your ad on the search engine results page for that specific keyword, your account is charged $1. If the amount of money in your account equals $1,000, then you can have 1,000 clicks on your ad before your account is depleted of funds.

However, if someone decides to target your ad via click fraud, they can use various methods to arrange to have your ad clicked on repeatedly until your $1,000 is gone. This can occur within a matter of minutes, or over a number of days or weeks, depending on the methods used and how blatant the fraudsters are about the process.

Obviously, this is an incredibly destructive type of fraud, especially since it occurs online, where many people feel they are acting anonymously. Some click fraud campaigns do not even attempt to hide their location or identity when making a lightning attack on your ad; instead, they wait and change their online "identity" after they have made a significant dent in your account or drained it altogether.

The Growth of Click Fraud

Excessive clicking on links to websites and forms of online advertising not tied to a cost-per-click payment is nothing new to the online community. Ever since the beginning of the Internet as a commercial enterprise, excessive clicking on search engine listings was used to create a sense of "popularity" of the website, which could lead to improved rankings of a site on the search engine (Stefanie Olsen, "Exposing Click Fraud").

It is partly because of this early type of questionable clicking that search engines began to explore different methods of ranking websites, leading eventually to today's reliance on complex algorithms, robot crawls, the infamous Google Dance, relevancy ratings, related links, content, popularity, and so on.

Likewise, repeated clicking on paid advertising where the advertiser pays for each click on their ad is not a recent development, but it has become a major problem for all parties involved.

This phenomenon, now referred to as "click fraud," has been a part of the Internet for quite some time. One of the earliest successful strikes against this type of fraud was conducted by Jessie C. Stricchiola, President of Alchemist Media, Inc., who identified and successfully procured a refund on behalf of the national corporation Chase Law Group against Goto.com (now Yahoo! Search Marketing) late in the year 2001.

It wasn't until later in 2002, however, that individuals and companies began to discuss the issue actively in online articles and forums. One of the main problems with combating click fraud then became apparent and remains so to this day—there are so many different interests, all with their own individual agenda, involved in the issue.

Of course advertisers are concerned that their ad dollars are being wasted by fraudulent clicks. At the same time, if an advertiser is also an affiliate, some see the potential in making back some of their own click fraud losses by practicing click fraud themselves on their affiliate sites.

Search engines, on the other hand, are interested in maximizing ad revenues (which click fraud accomplishes for them), yet realize that if they don't help to control click fraud, eventually they will lose advertisers and ad revenue.

Making the situation more complex, some people involved in perpetrating click fraud don't even understand that what they are doing is wrong. This is particularly true of those individuals who are not very computer literate or those who justify their actions because they themselves have been victims of click fraud.

In some cases, those involved have even been told they are helping the very people whose ad dollars they are depleting, because clicking on their ads increases the popularity of the website.

Click fraud didn't really become a huge problem until pay-per-click advertising became more popular and prevalent as a means of online advertising. Logic dictates that if there is nothing to practice click fraud upon, it is unlikely to be a large problem. Unfortunately, the increased popularity of pay-per-click advertising has invigorated the practice of fraudulently clicking on paid advertising.

Although many suspected fraudulent clicks were depleting PPC ad accounts, it wasn't until a few landmark cases that the online advertising industry reacted to the growing problem.

Probably the most infamous and audacious click-fraud case, which caught the attention of the industry and first alerted them to the scope of the potential danger of click fraud, involved an individual named Michael Anthony Bradley. Mr. Bradley developed a software program that he called "Google Clique." He claimed that the program allowed clicking on pay-per-click ads in such as way as to be virtually undetectable to search engines.

Bradley told Google that if they were not interested in purchasing his software at a reported price of $100,000, he would send copies of it to at least 100 spammers worldwide. This would result in fraud in the neighborhood of at least $5 million in the course of six months. Bradley was charged with extortion and wire fraud in March of 2004.

Later in the year, another significant lawsuit brought to the forefront another type of click fraud, this time involving affiliates. On November 15, 2004 Google sued one of the advertisers on its AdSense program (which involves websites including a PPC ad on their site in return for a portion of the income earned by Google when someone clicks on that ad).

The lawsuit claimed that Auctions Expert International, a Houston, Texas-based company, "flagrantly abused (Google) by artificially and/or fraudulently generating ad clicks …. These clicks were worthless to advertisers, but generated significant and unjust revenue for defendants." Key to the lawsuit was the claim by Google that the site itself was set up specifically for the purpose of click fraud and was never intended to be a legitimate auction website.

As for the search engines, many have begun to institute click fraud detection programs. Google itself claims that both the Bradley case and the Auctions International lawsuit show that Google is sending a warning to all who participate in click fraud that they "… have sophisticated technology that detects and eliminates fraud …. This lawsuit … demonstrates the success of our antifraud system and that we will take legal action when appropriate." (Steve Langdon, Google spokesperson)

These early high-profile legal cases are, however, just the tip of the iceberg in terms of click fraud in general. The largest challenge on this issue to date was a class action suit launched by Lane Gifts and Collectibles in February 2005 against a number of search engines, although Google early on became the defendant of most interest.

Click Fraud and How to Counteract It in Ad Campaigns

The $90 million settlement by Google late in July 2006 (of which one-third goes to the legal team) included a denial of the claims and any admission of legal liability or wrongdoing on the part of Google.

The settlement payments for those individuals who applied to be a part of the class action suit are just now (November 2006) being received. In general, recipients are not satisfied that the settlement they are receiving is in proportion to the cost of click fraud to them (one company reportedly has invested $480,000 over the last 3 years in PPC and received a credit of $280).

Estimates of the extent of the problem today vary widely, and this is a subject of much discussion among advertisers and PPC search engines. In 2005, estimates ranged from a low of 10% to as much as 50% or more of clicks falling into the fraudulent category.

Not surprisingly, search engines usually claim that, although a significant problem, it falls toward the lower percentage, while software and tool developers of anti-click-fraud measures lean toward the higher figure.

The first reliable statistical reports, released in early spring of 2006, surprised many in the industry. The reports indicated an overall click fraud percentage of about 15% of all clicks.

Recall, however, that many search engines have begun to filter out blatant click fraud efforts (such as repeated clicking from the same IP address

> Click fraud is estimated to be between 10% and 30% of all PPC advertising spending.

within a too-short period of time to be reasonable)—so this 15% is the proportion of clicks that are estimated to be fraudulent after the search engines have already scrubbed the data.

One thing all agree on is that click fraud has been a problem in the past and that it is becoming a greater problem now.

Left to flourish on its own, click fraud ultimately could bring the entire pay-per-click industry to a halt, with advertisers losing enough money on ad campaigns to drop their ROIs to negative numbers. This, in turn, could lead them to withdraw from PPC advertising altogether.

Since most search engines rely on paid advertising as a prime source of their income, they have an equally large incentive and stake in ultimately bringing click fraud statistics down to the lowest possible percentage.

As long as there are people willing to commit fraud, however, click fraud will never be eliminated. Advertisers and search engines agree, however, that the issue needs to be addressed now, before it gets completely out of hand.

How Click Fraud Affects Advertisers

In addition to draining individual ad campaign accounts, click fraud contributes to the overall increase in the cost per click for keywords.

Many PPC search engines base keyword pricing on how popular a term is and how many people are competing for it. Therefore, if click fraud is directed at a certain keyword, the cost of that keyword can increase for all advertisers, not just the particular competitor who may have been the target of the click fraud attack.

One of the most promising developments, as far as advertisers are concerned, has been the foundation of The Click Fraud Network, an initiative begun by Click Forensics to track as much internet activity as possible and, using tools developed by those who struggle with click fraud, come up with some answers to the questions surrounding the problem.

By analyzing and cataloging as much search activity as their members generate, the Click Fraud Network hopes to provide statistically significant reports on click fraud that advertisers can trust in making decisions.

The involvement by the Interactive Advertising Bureau (IAB) in the issue of click fraud through the foundation of the Measurement Task Force mid-year has added more credibility to the process. A task force composed of dozens of industry analysts and experts contribute their expertise and opinions to issues such as actually defining what a "click" is, what might make the definition of a "click" different in a PPC advertisement than it is in a search listing, and putting a lot more flesh on the skeleton of the infamous Google term "invalid click". Google, Yahoo!, MSN and Ask.com are among the search engines with membership on the committee.

What About That Infamous "Invalid Click"? How Is It Defined?

As a quick point of reference, the following are the Big 4's "official" definitions of invalid clicks or what they consider as click fraud.

Google

"What are invalid clicks? Invalid clicks are clicks generated by prohibited methods. Examples of invalid clicks may include repeated manual clicking or the use of robots, automated clicking tools, or other deceptive software. Invalid clicks are sometimes intended to artificially and/or maliciously drive up an advertiser's clicks and or a publisher's earnings. Sources of invalid clicks may include: manual clicks intended to increase your advertising costs or to increase profits for website owners hosting your ads and/or clicks by automated tools, robots, or other deceptive software".

Yahoo! Search Marketing

"Yahoo! Search Marketing wants advertisers to understand that traffic quality and click fraud are two very different things. Click fraud is generally considered to be clicks made with bad faith with the sole purpose of generating a charge to the advertiser with zero possibility of a legitimate site visit or transaction occurring. We agree. But from a technical perspective, it is impossible to look into someone's mind at the time they click to see whether they are clicking with bad faith. In other words, we can't read users' minds. Instead, Yahoo! Search Marketing has to look at what identifiable behavior may indicate bad faith. In terms of identifiable behavior, we define click fraud as detected illegitimate bots and certain repetitive clicks. And we have created sophisticated software that identifies this behavior and attempts to filter out charges for these clicks so that you are not billed for them. We do not disclose how we define repetitive clicks or the details about our proprietary technology because we do not want to educate those who are acting in bad faith."

Microsoft adCenter

"A. What is an invalid click? An invalid click is a click that Microsoft adCenter has identified as having characteristics typical of user error, malicious activity, or similar types of irregular activity."

Ask.com

"Clicks can be marked as valid or invalid. Valid clicks are clicks on a listing that are generated by humans, whose intent we judge to be to engage the advertiser's site (such as to make a purchase, register for services, or navigate content.). Invalid clicks are clicks generated by robots, systems or software whose intent we judge not to be to engage the advertiser's site."

So, a large part of each definition of click fraud is still left to the search engine's discretion—as indicated by phrasing such as: "whose intent we have judged", "that [our office] has identified as having characteristics of"; "we do not disclose ... the details about our proprietary technology", "clicks generated by prohibited methods."

Everyone involved wants a solution to the problem (with the possible exception of those whose livelihood depends upon click fraud success) and the increased visibility of organizations and providers of PPC speaking out to define the issues is a big step forward towards a workable solution.

The Sources of Click Fraud

So far, we've alluded to different types of click fraud, but a complete breakdown of the most prevalent sources and forms of click fraud may assist in clarifying the range and potential impact different methods of click fraud have and why it is such a complex issue.

Types of click fraud range from the simple and direct to the complex and sophisticated. Here are some of the most common forms of click fraud.

1. **Automated Scripts**—although not the simplest form of click fraud, for someone with computer expertise, this method can be very effective and quite simple to set up. The most famous case of this type of click fraud is still the Google Clique software. Basically, the fraudster creates a robot or automated script that is specifically designed to click on paid advertising. This type of click fraud is used by both competitors and affiliates alike.

2. **Hiring People to Click on Ads**—this means of perpetrating click fraud often originates from third-world countries. Ads are placed in local newspapers recruiting workers to spend time clicking on ads, according to directions supplied by the companies who organize these operations. The most infamous operation of this type of "click farm" was identified by The Times of India in an article entitled "India's Secret Army of Ad Clickers" in 2005.

   Although those operating "click farms" obviously realize that they are committing fraud, those working for them do not necessarily understand the significance of what they are doing, nor the impact it has on overall Internet commercial activity. In third-world countries where annual incomes average a few thousand dollars, the additional income of $100 to $200 per month for a few hours work per day is very hard to resist, especially if the individuals involved are not computer literate enough to realize the implications of their actions. Some have even been told they are helping increase the market visibility of a company by clicking on their ads repeatedly.

3. **Competitors**—your competitors have many methods of generating click fraud that do not involve "hitbots" or "click farms." If you are competing for position on PPC search engines for a particularly expensive keyword, all a competitor has to do is to click on your ad a couple of times a day from his office computer, his home computer, a laptop, a friend's computer, an Internet café, or any variety of easily accessed computers with different IP addresses in order to deplete your account and not attract attention.

   In competitive industries, where the cost per click can be several dollars, if three to five of your competitors make fraudulent clicks on your ad several times a day, you can easily be losing thousands of advertising dollars a month.

If your keyword cost is in the lower range, click fraud by your competitor(s) needs to be a little more complex and sophisticated than simply a few extra clicks here and there to be effective.

4. **Proxy Servers**—one of the most basic means of click fraud involves the use of repeated clicks on a PPC ad from the same computer. A person could theoretically sit at their computer and click on your ad, wait the amount of time for the PPC search engine to consider it a legitimate click, perhaps even visit a few of your pages and then exit your website. Bingo! One clickthrough deducted from your account.

   There are cases where people will complete this process repeatedly, without even bothering to go through the simple process of changing their IP address (the Internet Protocol number that is assigned to each computer). However, people using this click fraud tactic use proxy servers to allow new, randomized IP addresses to be generated at specific intervals in order to make it appear as if the clicks are indeed coming from different computers.

5. **Affiliate Programs**—affiliates are an increasing source of click fraud. Because affiliates receive a percentage of the money generated by each click made on their website, they may see little or no harm in clicking a couple of times on the ad themselves to generate a little extra income on the side.

   However, affiliates who use "bots" to generate significant revenue via click fraud usually have to develop fairly sophisticated technology to get past the filters that many of the PPC search engines have in place for programs such as Google AdSense.

6. **Impression Fraud**—Usually via a robot, your competitor visits your website through normal means (not by clicking on your paid ad), thus artificially inflating your impressions and causing your clickthrough rate to drop. On Google, if your clickthrough rate results in a Quality Score reduction sufficient to kick it below the rate needed to remain active, your ad may be disabled and your competitor can grab a top position at a much lower keyword cost.

   A secondary result of this type of fraud is that your website may be seen by the search engine as becoming less relevant, since you are getting a lot of impressions without clicks, which could ultimately lead to a shutdown of your ad campaign. Google recently added the quality of your landing pages into the mix of what goes into defining a "Quality Score" for your site.

These are just some of the more common means of click fraud. Some suspect activity may indeed be click fraud, but is subtle enough to be impossible to label it as such. To do so, one must know the intent of the searcher—did they just find it more convenient to go back to the page with your PPC ad on it and click there to get to your website than remembering your URL?

Click fraud is definitely sometimes difficult to track, and innocent actions can sometimes be misinterpreted as click fraud. People do mistakenly click on an ad when they don't intend to and some people find it easier to click on a PPC ad to find out a company's phone number than to consult an online yellow pages directory.

So how can you tell if you are a victim of click fraud, given that its very nature is somewhat amorphous?

Detecting Click Fraud

Some telltale signs of click fraud are quite obvious, while others take a little more tracking and analysis to identify. Many PPC search engines have programs in place to audit for click fraud, which we'll discuss later in this chapter, but it is a good policy to periodically look at your traffic logs, or perhaps consider using a third-party tool to analyze the data further.

The main things to look for in your ad campaign's statistics are:

1. **Keyword performance**—if you notice that some specific keywords in your ad campaign that normally do not do well suddenly become top performers, investigate. If you suspect click fraud, begin by changing the setup of your ad campaigns so that you can track each keyword by search engine and then keep an eye on the statistics of each (now) separate campaign. In this way, you can see more clearly if one specific search engine is involved. As well, the data is broken down in more manageable portions, so that repeated visits by the same IP address may stand out more clearly than if you kept all your keyword campaigns in one log file.

    Likewise, a sudden increase in the total number of clicks on all of your keywords, without a seasonal relationship or a special promotional campaign in progress, could indicate click fraud.

2. **An abnormal number of clicks from the same IP address**— although this is the most obvious and easily identified form of click fraud, it is amazing how many fraudsters still use this method, particularly for quick attacks. They may choose to strike over a long weekend when they figure you may not be watching your log files carefully. Then they repeatedly click on your ad so that, when you return to work on Tuesday, your account is significantly depleted.

3. **Decline in the number of conversions**—if your conversion rate is normally positive (that is, you are making a profit on your ad), and

suddenly conversion dives into negative numbers, this could be a sign of click fraud in action. Click fraud results in extra clicks on your ad with no actual purchases, and your conversion rate will fall accordingly.

4. **Large numbers of visitors who leave your site quickly**—another indication of click fraud can be a pattern of visitors clicking on your ad, spending the minimum amount of time on your site required by your PPC search engine to establish it as a valid click (usually 30 seconds or more), and then leaving without having left the landing page.

5. **A large number of impressions, without the accompanying click on your ad**—if you notice that there are a lot more impressions (views) of your website; this could indicate the impression fraud we discussed earlier. As we saw, artificial inflation of your ad impressions may cause your clickthrough rates to drop below the Google minimum Quality Score for your keywords, and your ad may be disabled. Until you realize this, your competitors have free reign to use your keywords, sometimes at bargain prices. In addition, your relevancy ratings for search engines may drop as they record numerous impressions, but no interest shown via visits to other parts of your website. This could ultimately lead to a shutdown of your campaign.

6. **Abnormally high clicks and impressions on affiliate websites**—although affiliates are themselves sometimes involved in conducting click fraud schemes, they can be victims of click fraud themselves. If one of their competitors uses this same method of excessive clicks and impressions on an affiliate's site, the PPC search engine will soon notice an abnormally high payment to a certain affiliate and perhaps go as far as canceling that affiliate's account, even though he or she was not engaging in any form of click fraud.

7. **A large number of clicks coming from countries outside of your normal market area**—using online resources such as www.dnsstuff.com and other free online sites, you can identify which country an IP address is probably coming from.

8. **Accidental click fraud**—there are, in fact, some cases that may be seen as click fraud, but are actually unintentional. In the past, for example, double-clicks on a PPC ad used to be counted as 2 clicks, even though the user was just performing a typical double-click in response to seeing a link. Accidental as they may be, they still deplete your ad account.

Although some individuals may accidentally click on your ad, most accidental clicks are caused by link-checking software or search engine robots clicking on the ad as they run their routines. If you suspect this is occurring, regular log checks may be all you need to get a refund from your PPC search engine. With spider-driven extra clicks, if you have a high-cost keyword in your campaign, even a few extra clicks a day can make a dent in your account.

There are other means of click fraud that individuals use, but most fall into the above categories. Most people believe that the majority of the real damage is done by robot-driven software, but it is impossible to adequately determine what percentage of click fraud is caused by humans themselves and what percentage is caused by robots that humans developed.

One of the main reasons that robot/software click fraud is so prevalent is that there are actually legitimate pieces of software that can be used to commit click fraud, although such was not the original intent for their creation. For example, a click fraud artist may claim that he is just stress testing his analytics software program to ensure that it will catch click fraud.

The difficulty is that, even if you suspect you are a victim of click fraud, the onus generally falls on you to prove that it exists and to find those responsible. This must happen before any action will be taken by your PPC search engine, especially those that already have some form of click fraud detection operating on their engines. So, just exactly what will your PPC search engine do if you make a claim of click fraud?

The Response of Search Engines to Click Fraud

We've spoken briefly about PPC search engines and how they have responded to various incidents of click fraud. Not all search engines have programs in place that routinely check ad accounts for warning signs of click fraud, but more and more engines are instituting such programs in light of the increasing incidence of click fraud and pressure from their advertisers to deal with the problem.

> Click fraud is currently one of the largest threats to the survival and growth of pay-per-click search engines.

The two largest search engines—Google and Yahoo!—both have publicly admitted that click fraud is a problem that is a significant threat, not just to their "business model," but to their overall success.

At this point, the response of Google to click fraud is a touch more detailed and drills down further into the raw data than Yahoo! Still, both search engines have proprietary systems in place that are constantly being upgraded as new methods of click fraud become apparent and the level of detected click fraud increases.

Consumers expect to see some results from the industry-wide initiatives under the IAB banner and as reports from the independent Click Network Group accumulate, providing the industry with more information to find solutions to the problem.

Although all search engines are very tight-lipped about revealing how much they have refunded to advertisers on click-fraud claims, Google has refunded money lost by advertisers, and publishers have had their payments adjusted if they are suspected of affiliate-related fraud. In addition, the November 2004 lawsuit by Google against Auctions International indicates that they are willing to take legal action in cases they consider worthy of such action.

Despite their stated good intentions, and evidence of quick action on claims by advertisers of suspected click fraud, many advertisers feel that Google is not doing enough to combat the problem. Many are frustrated in their attempts to reach the level of proof that Google expects to qualify for a refund. It is in this search engine's best interests to keeps its advertisers happy, but it is a complex problem.

Yahoo! Search Marketing, like Google, has proprietary software designed to detect click fraud. This software has been refined on a regular basis since 1998, and now checks at least 50 points of data, from the more obvious ones, such as IP addresses, cookie information, or the visitor's browser's information, to more sophisticated recognition of patterns of behavior on individual websites. If the cumulative number of data points concludes that the activity is invalid, the advertiser is not charged for the click (although Yahoo! is unable to remove the information from the advertiser's logs, leading some to question how far Yahoo! is actually going to combat click fraud).

Yahoo! also encourages advertisers to report suspicious behavior found in ad activity, and will investigate further and issue refunds when appropriate. Keep in mind that if your claim is denied, you should appeal and get them to take it seriously. In fact, experience has shown that if you keep appealing and appealing these rulings, eventually your chances of reaching someone who will look into the situation with a realistic viewpoint are increased, so don't give up after a first refusal of your request for a refund.

Some other PPC search engines also have formalized systems in place to detect click fraud, such as LookSmart's TrueLead™ system. Other PPC search engines, however, may not have formal click fraud systems in place, but do monitor traffic on an informal basis. All will consider any claims made by an advertiser based on an allegation of click fraud.

How Advertisers Can Combat Click Fraud

Unfortunately, because so many PPC search engines have yet to establish any formalized programs to detect click fraud—and those that have only detect a portion of actual fraud—the responsibility to proactively combat click fraud still falls on the advertiser.

A big problem with this is the amount of time involved in analyzing and organizing click fraud evidence to present to the PPC search engine in order to seek a refund. Sometimes, the time involved in following through on such a claim costs more than the actual dollars involved in the click fraud itself, which causes many in that position to remain quiet, something that click fraud operators count on to stay operational.

> Many third-party tools exist to help advertisers monitor and track their campaigns for click fraud and assist them with getting their money back from search engines.

However, if you are already using tracking software for web analytics (a recommended step for any PPC campaign), use that information to identify potential click fraud. Some tracking software even includes a click-fraud detection component.

Third-party tools specifically designed to look for signs of click fraud and help analyze your log files to find out if you have been a victim are widely available. Such tools can also lend some credibility with your PPC search engine if you discover a problem and take it to the search engine for a refund. Some companies will even take your case to the search engine for you.

We'll discuss some of the third-party tools for combating click fraud in the upcoming chapter on pay-per-click tools. There are many available including www.AdWatcher.com and www.Clicklab.com. More and more products have found their way to the market, as the problem of click fraud continues to gain even more notoriety and search engines and advertisers work together and separately for solutions.

Besides relying on the search engines themselves, using a third-party tool, and engaging in some manual checking yourself, what else can you do to combat click fraud and receive compensation from the PPC search engine?

One step you can take is to disable any content search function you have and then keep track of your statistics while relying solely on the PPC search engine ads to test if affiliates may be involved in click fraud. If your data shows a rapid decline in the amount of suspect clicks, turn content search back on and see if the clickthroughs reappear. Documentation of this type of experiment is great evidence to provide to the search engine to back up your claims of affiliate click fraud.

Another very effective method, suggested by a third-party tool, is to use their software to activate a customizable popup message that will appear on the user's computer screen if they click a certain number of times on your paid ad within a certain time period. For example, if someone clicks five times on your paid ad within the space of an hour, they will see a popup message, very politely written, stating something to the effect that their repeat visits have been noticed and inviting them to contact you if they are having difficulty finding what they are looking for. This innocuous-looking warning sign works quite well at deterring a number of basic-level fraudsters.

Suspicious Behavior Detected!
Your internet location has been detected visiting this site more than 5 times over the past 24 hours. Your information has been logged and sent to the owner of the advertising campaign.

We appreciate your interest and thank you for your visits. However, to protect our customers from higher prices by keeping advertising dollars down, we routinely examine recurrent visitations from their advertising campaigns.

Please help us pass the savings on to you by bookmarking our site for future reference.

Thank you for visiting and enjoy browsing our site!

IP: 67.100.XXX.XX - Agent: IE 6.x and above

Figure 6.1 – When a fraud-monitoring service notices suspicious behavior, it shows a message such as this to the potential fraudster before redirecting them to the actual landing page.

It is very important to keep accurate and complete records of any reports or statistical analyses (either print versions or screenshots) of suspicious data.

If your logs show that the same IP address is clicking on your ad 24 times each day, having a hard copy documenting that occurrence will go a long way toward proving your case to the search engine in question.

Likewise, if you can document the occurrence of click fraud on certain pages, you may be able to narrow down the potential perpetrators, especially if you suspect affiliate click fraud.

If you feel you have adequate proof of click fraud, you should contact the search engine involved directly via email, attaching the proof you have collected and any further details or evidence supporting your claim.

Another possible tactic, if you are a relatively small business and have fairly clear evidence that a competitor is the instigator of the majority of your losses, is to place a carefully worded, simple phone call or email to them outlining your observations. This may be enough to stop the problem. You could also contact a third competitor to see if they are having a similar problem, and perhaps combine forces to combat the problem more effectively.

No matter how you choose to deal with a potential click fraud problem, while the investigation is ongoing, continue to monitor your paid advertising statistics carefully and diligently to ward off further attacks and to enable your monitoring of the actions your search engine is taking to resolve the matter.

As with tracking ad campaigns, dealing with click fraud all comes down to one process—tracking, tracking, and then more tracking.

In the next chapter, we'll discuss advertising for the content network versus the search network—how they differ from more common, search-driven PPC listings, and unique aspects advertisers must know and keep in mind if they choose to invest in these forms of advertising.

Chapter 7 – The Role of Relevance:
PPC Contextual and Search Advertising

So far, we have discussed standard pay-per-click ads directed at the "search" market, or ads placed on search engine results pages (SERPs) only. Throughout 2006, however, ad placement has become more complex. On the one hand, more options mean greater choices for advertisers; however, search engines have managed to rework some of the defining concepts of PPC advertising and seize back a measure of control, in the name of "relevancy" and a "good customer experience."

What began as two different types of PPC advertising—one based on a formula approach to keyword bidding and the other based on content as a measure of relevancy—has led to a different situation. Up until recently, deciding whether to choose the "search" or the "content" network when setting up your Google AdWords account was a defining moment; today, different issues are crucial—such as the quality of the landing page users clicking on your ad wind up on.

The market has changed from one where the advertiser tells the search engine what he/she is willing to pay for ad placement to one where search engines tell you if the price you are willing to pay is enough for your ad to appear.

Factors involved, aside from bid price, include the perceived quality of the content of your website, the quality of in-bound links to your site, how relevant the content is to the topic of your ad and—the most recent addition to the algorithm—a measure of the quality and relevance of your proposed landing page.

Not all search engines have reached this point yet—many still operate a standard, auction-based concept. For the larger engines, the lever of control is moving back towards unfathomable algorithms and "formulas" to decide keyword pricing. Google states plainly and repeatedly that if your keywords are inactive for search, you should concentrate on optimizing your keywords, ad, and landing page BEFORE you increase your maximum cost-per-click figure upwards.

Let's look a little closer at the details of this change in approach. Given its command of the online advertising marketplace and its pivotal role in changing the PPC landscape, Google is undeniably the search engine to look at regarding the growth of contextual advertising vis-à-vis the search market alone.

Yahoo! is on the verge of implementing a similar structure (via its upcoming Panama model) and Microsoft is currently running a content-oriented advertising pilot program. Other, smaller search engines have variations of content-influenced placement of ads in use as well.

Quality Score—Google Changes Tactics

Google set the search advertising world on its ear in 2006 by officially integrating a measure they dubbed "quality score" into PPC advertising. The basics of opening, running and optimizing an ad campaign remain pretty much the same. However, the focus has shifted from a bid-based auction setup to one of assigning eligibility for placement depending upon the content, quality and relevance of your website and landing pages. This judgment of eligibility is a prerequisite to taking part in bidding for keywords.

In essence, an advertiser can be willing to pay as much as necessary to secure a PPC placement, but Google can (and will) stop that advertiser from participating in AdWords if they deem that the site and campaign are not up to the standards they have set. You can tell if your keywords have been accepted or not by checking to see if they are marked as "active for search" or "inactive for search" in your account.

The advent of Quality Score and other changes to the PPC process resulted in a number of sites seeing their ads drop completely off the map overnight, resulting in a scramble to re-work ads, keywords, and websites in order to rejoin the bidding.

The motive behind Quality Score is multi-dimensional, but one important aspect was Google's wish to provide a quality user experience, and the emphasis on relevant content was, to some degree, aimed at link farms and link arbitrage practitioners.

Those involved in such controversial practices have already begun to counter the changes to the algorithms of Google. They are implementing cloaking pages, for example, to serve up different content to search engine spiders than is presented when one clicks on a PPC ad. They are willing to risk banning in order to continue profitable schemes, but most SEOs would caution against such risky practices.

What prompted Google and other search engines to place such importance on content in the PPC advertising process? Content-based advertising is a technique that has a history going back to the beginnings of the commercial base of the web, but last year (2006) vaulted it to the pinnacle of success, as search engines realized that ordinary people searching for something on the Internet are interested in quality results as quickly as possible.

If a searcher does not find what they want on a site within a few seconds, they will go to another, and another, and another; if the search engine they are using isn't providing them with quality sites just as quickly, they may try another search engine. Thus, the lifeblood of the search engines (advertising) has to appeal to user wishes as well as the requirements of the search engines themselves.

First, let's explore the differences between using the search and the content network for placement of PPC advertising—what you should be looking for and considering when making judgments about where to set up your campaigns.

Choosing Between Search Results and Content Network Placement

What makes contextual advertising (usually referred to as advertising on the "content network") different is that ads do not appear on search engine result pages. Rather, they appear directly on pages of content found on websites. In effect, if you visit a website that has information about digital cameras, you may encounter contextual advertising of related products such as memory cards, camera cases, zoom lenses, battery rechargers, etc.

Although many analysts consider contextual advertising to be a new phenomenon, it has been present, mainly in the form of banner advertising, popups, and other ads, since the Internet became a commercial enterprise.

In the past, some consumers considered these means of advertising undesirable and even an unwanted part of their search experience, viewing them as unnecessary clutter that detracted from the actual information available on a web page.

For example, most of us have had the experience of visiting a website and then being prompted to allow the download of software, which, once installed on your computer, will allow contextual ads in the form of popups, and the like to be shown as you travel through various websites.

If your computer is not set up to prompt you before downloading software, you may actually have such programs installed on your computer, without even knowing it. Sometimes these types of programs encourage the visitor to download the software by offering free benefits, such as access to coupon sites or dictionary/encyclopedia resources. Such programs are typically called spyware or adware and are regarded very negatively among online users.

By the year 2003, contextual advertising had become a form of advertising that consumers did not generally respond well to, and many users began to install popup-blocking software to cut down on the incidence of unwanted ads suddenly appearing in a new window or as part of the current browser window.

However, also in 2003, a change in public perception of contextual advertising allowed it to become a means of capturing new traffic for advertisers. With spyware and adware deemed unacceptable, it became apparent that another thing differentiating PPC contextual advertising from PPC search advertising is not just how and where it appears, but also the type of user it appeals to.

PPC contextual advertising is designed to appear on pages of a website that have content that is highly relevant to the ad. Depending on which search engine is delivering the advertising, the ads may appear on the right, top, or bottom side of the web page, and be similar in appearance to standard PPC ads, with a title, description, and URL to click on.

The types of websites that typically carry contextual ads are news sites, magazine sites, educational sites, product review sites and other reference sites. Google also places content ads in their email service (Gmail) and in some newsletters that meet the requirements Google has placed upon them.

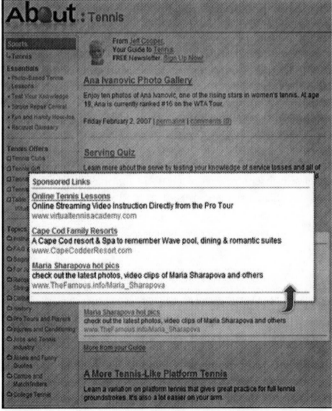

There is little-to-no incentive for an advertiser to add contextual ads to their websites, as their competitor's own ads could wind up being shown there as well.

While contextual ads are primarily textual in nature, advertisers should consider including images, to afford themselves of the opportunity to showcase products as well as a link to their website—a move considered to add more "relevance" to your offering.

Figure 7.1. – Contextual ads (for tennis-related products) by Google appear on a content site about tennis.

Content ads tend to be clicked on by visitors who are in a different stage of the buying cycle and may not be interested in purchasing a product at all.

> Content ads generally deliver a lower ROI because they are clicked on by people in a different stage of the buying process, as compared to regular search clicks.

Because they appear in the websites of, for example, online newspapers, a contextual ad may be shown just because the text of the article mentions the type of product, even if the intent of the article has nothing to do with selling that product.

The person reading the article may have no intention of purchasing that product at that time but may, out of curiosity, click on the contextual ad just to see what it's talking about and get a little more information about a product they may not know much about.

Pay-per-click ads on a search engine, however, are more often clicked by visitors who are interested in purchasing the product in question. Although many may still be in the research phase, they more often than not have a purchase in mind.

Therefore, contextual ads usually have a lower conversion rate or ROI than search pay-per-click ads, because of the intent of the visitor clicking on the ad. Nevertheless, the contextual ad campaign is still charged for each click on the ad, although the cost per click for the same keyword may in fact be less than on the search model.

Despite some earlier reservations about the conversion quality on content advertising, the move by search engines to place more emphasis on content in judging websites and ads for placement in organic or paid results has inevitably led to more and more advertisers moving to contextual advertising.

Aside from search engine pressure, positive factors of this approach have contributed to its growth:

♦ Contextual ads tend to have more online exposure than search pay-per-click ads, because their placement on partner sites of the search engine is determined by their relevance to the content of those sites, and is not totally dependent upon keyword bidding to achieve placement.

♦ Contextual ads are a good source of revenue for partner sites that include them. Because the ads are not in competition with the "product" being offered by the content website, they are generally seen as a plus by content partners.

Further Developments Enhancing the Appeal of Advertising on the "Content Network"

Content advertising became a familiar commodity to many webmasters through the Google AdSense program, which allows publishers and website owners to place Google ads on their sites and share in the profits from clicks made to those ads. The vision at Google was to use contextual search as a means of delivering more relevant ads to its network of partners and advertisers.

Google was one of the first search engines to offer content targeting in their AdSense program, which launched in March of 2003. AdSense initially limited those eligible to participate to its larger partnered websites (those with a minimum of 20 million page views per month).

It wasn't until June of 2003 that Google expanded the program to allow smaller sites to participate and simplified the sign-up process, so that a publisher could sign up online.

Google has positioned content search as a means for advertisers to have their ads automatically appear on highly relevant websites, stating that the program will increase an advertiser's ROI and reach, and save them time and money via their "extensive network of high-quality partner sites and products."

In fact, contextual advertising was more suited to the Google AdSense program, because its main purpose is to increase revenue for publishers by providing relevant ads for their websites prior to the onset of "Quality Score" and the prime important of relevancy of content. Google felt that by providing targeted advertising throughout a website (particularly small websites with small advertising budgets), sites would benefit from increased traffic, while advertisers would benefit from visitor clicks on the ad and visits to their site.

> Sites with content about gambling, pornography, or drugs are not allowed into the contextual advertising program in any way.

The content program is robust enough to differentiate between meanings of common words, such as "mouse" as either an animal or a computer peripheral device, and thereby not serve up an ad for a computer mouse ad on a medical research website. It also has a filtering process to eliminate matching ads with articles reporting bad news; thus, not placing car ads on content pages discussing a recent car crash, for example.

Some degree of manual review of potential matches of ad to content is also in place, in addition to the automated placement method.

Google also allows advertisers to block specific URLs they do not want to appear on their site, thus eliminating the risk of a competitor's ad showing up on their website. Conversely, one can target your ads to specific sites only, or only one site, if you so desire.

And, most recently, Google announced those without websites can tie their PPC ad to a content page hosted by Google that will provide information about your business and contact directions (in effect, a one-page mini-site requiring no HTML experience, allowing at least one image to appear, but relatively limited in individualization techniques).

Google Analytics is a free adjunct to PPC advertising, as are different monitoring tools and reports, which include the clickthrough rate, the number of impressions, and the number of clicks. You can also group results by URL, ad type, domain name, category, and other parameters.

Earnings from contextual advertising are displayed and easily accessed separately from results from search ads, so you can quickly check how much revenue they are generating and then make decisions about changes easily and in a timely manner.

Soon after Google began offering contextual advertising, competitors jumped on the bandwagon. By July of 2003, Yahoo! had developed its answer to Google—Content Match. Content Match offers the same features as the Google contextual ad program, but delivers results to different partners.

The Yahoo! Search Marketing program concentrates more on involving its major partners, such as Yahoo!, CNN, ESPN, and MSN, in contextual advertising. Fewer tools are offered by the Yahoo! program to date, although the upcoming Panama platform change will see a system much more closely akin to the Google model than previously.

The other leading search engine, Microsoft Live Search (formerly MSN), is experimenting with a pilot project that sets up advertising models along the lines of SERPs ads and content-based ads, again much like the Google model.

A couple of other PPC search engines that offer content/contextual search include:

- Seevast (parent company of Kanoodle.com) and its products under the brand name Pulse360 (ads may appear on partners such as MSNBC, The Wall Street Journal, Fox.com, MarketWatch/Dow Jones).

- MIVA (formerly FindWhat.com), which comes in two flavors—an automated version and one the advertiser controls manually.

In addition, a number of web properties offer a form of contextual advertising, although the network of websites that content-related ads may appear on is much smaller.

Some examples to investigate include:

♦ www.Clicksor.com

♦ www.BidClix.com

♦ www.Bidvertiser.com

♦ www.AdBrite.com

♦ www.Quigo.com - The AdSonar Exchange

When Contextual Pay-Per-Click Advertising Is a Good Choice

There are a lot of factors an advertiser should consider before deciding on contextual versus keyword-based search pay-per-click options. However, the best way to quickly discover which factors may work in your favor, with either model, is to investigate the contextual marketplace by experimenting with your ongoing ad campaigns.

Before you begin any contextual search ad campaign, ensure that your keyword-based search ad setup is working at its optimal capacity. The first step is to ensure that the content tracking option is turned off, if you use Google or Yahoo! in your basic setup.

When you first open an account with these two search engines, "content search" is automatically set to the "on" position. However, if you are only interested in pay-per-click search ads, or you are going to test contextual advertising, you need to adjust these settings. You can find this setting on the basic setup page of your account.

Once you have turned content matching off, take some time and look at your keywords. Then track and analyze your data from the search network to ensure that you have your keywords positioned where you want them to be and that you are happy with the results you are getting from your PPC search campaign(s).

Add negative keywords where appropriate, and remove any keywords that aren't performing to your expectations. In effect, get your search-based pay-per-click ad campaign as close to perfection as possible, so that you will be able to make an accurate comparison between it and the contextual search version you will set up.

As an example of how to test contextual advertising, let's use the following scenario based on a Google account.

You will need to set up to three separate campaigns—one that will reveal your natural or organic search results, one that will show your pay-per-click ad campaign search results, and a final one that will show results from a pay-per-click contextual results ad campaign.

Using your base campaign, make two copies of the entire campaign, and then change the settings for "where to show my ad" to:

♦ One with neither box checked (this can be left out if you are not concerned about your natural ranking in search engines)

♦ One with "search network" only checked

♦ One with "content network" only checked

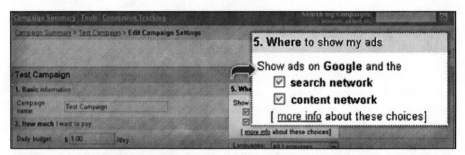

Figure 7.2. – You can edit where your ads appear on Google by going into "Campaign Summary," checking the campaigns you want to edit, and then clicking on "Edit Settings." You can set whether you want the ads to appear on Google only or be spread out over their search partners and AdSense publishers.

Ensure that you have individual tracking set up for every keyword in each of the three campaigns, with appropriate identifiers set up in the tracking URLs, so that you can analyze the data completely.

Set the campaigns to run at the same time and let them run for a reasonable amount of time—anywhere from a week to as long as a month—so that you can collect enough impressions on each separate campaign to have adequate data to analyze.

Once the ads have run long enough to generate sufficient data, stop the campaigns and then reactivate your original campaign.

At this point, you must analyze the data from the separate campaigns in order to determine whether PPC search ads resulted in more positive results than did the PPC contextual ads.

Although you can use the tracking tools available in Google to analyze the data, we recommend that you also use a third-party tool to compare the different analyses. If you do not own a third-party tool, some of the more popular ones do have trial periods available that would allow you to download the software and analyze the data from the test period. (Be aware that trial software often does not have the full features of the program enabled.)

Finally, look at the data yourself. Invest as much time as necessary to fully understand the different results you most likely received from the different ad campaigns, concentrating particularly on clickthrough rates and conversions.

If you discover that the campaigns received many impressions, but not as many clickthroughs as you had expected, you may need to revise your keywords and ads a little more. If this is the case, make some revisions, re-run the trials, and see if the results come out any clearer.

As stated earlier, most analysts say that contextual ads lead to fewer conversions than PPC search engine ads, due to the timing of when the visitor sees the ad, in terms of their stage in the buying cycle.

Those who reach your website via PPC search tend to be further along the sales cycle. This means that they are drilling down with more specific keywords and actively looking for businesses that sell the product they are searching for, in order to make the final decision.

Given this, many advertisers at first may see contextual advertising as a poor choice if their sole intent is to sell products online. However, there are some distinct advantages to be gained via contextual search advertising, as long as the advertiser realizes that conversions will likely be smaller.

One of the main advantages is that keywords in contextual advertising tend to cost less than keywords used in PPC search. Therefore, an ad campaign based on content can cost less, so fewer conversions can still result in a decent ROI.

Additionally, one cannot discount the exposure of your product and website in any format online, but particularly in content-rich pages. Typically, visitors who are reading such content online already have a high degree of interest in the topic. Therefore, they may be more likely to notice your ad or at least make note of your website as a possible avenue to explore when they are closer to the end of the sales cycle and ready to purchase.

This can be particularly beneficial to smaller websites, who face a great deal of difficulty in building brand recognition in the Internet marketplace. By attracting the attention of a reader who is already interested in the product, it may give a small business owner a leg up on larger competitors, who rely on their brand name to bring shoppers directly to their websites.

Another advantage of contextual advertising is that it may have more appeal to those Internet users who find the search process difficult and frustrating. If a user has tried to find the product he is looking for by placing keywords in a search engine search box and has repeatedly been unable to find relevant results, frustration will set in.

Some potential customers may instead click on the contextual results that come up, such as links to online magazines or review sites. If your ad shows up when they are investigating those secondary sites, their frustration at the whole process may lead them to click onto your ad and propel them further into the sales cycle on that basis alone.

Ultimately, however, the biggest deciding factor in whether or not to opt in to the content network is that Google (and most other search engines following its lead) is making content the key factor in all aspects of search, whether you are looking at content pages such as a magazine site or SERPs.

Organic results are being judged and ranked depending upon the relevancy of their content and paid advertising and sponsored results are following suit. It has almost reached the point where an advertiser will no longer have the choice of not advertising on the content network, but advertisers still need to track their campaigns and ensure that they are making the right choices, whatever they may be, for their individual products and services.

Tips and Techniques for Contextual Ads

The following are some tips and techniques to keep in mind as you explore the use of content ads in your PPC campaigns.

- ◆ If you are interested in exploring contextual ads, be sure that "content search" is turned on in your basic setup page of your account (in general, it's turned on by default). Conversely, ensure that "content search" is turned off if you are not interested in having your pay-per-click ads show up on content websites.

- ◆ Run competitive tests between your PPC search and your PPC contextual search ads before committing yourself to one or the other exclusively.

- ◆ Contextual ads have a different purpose than pay-per-click search ads—they are designed to instill interest in the product, while PPC search ads focus on conversions. Thus, consider developing different landing pages and ad descriptions for each type of advertising.

♦ Keep in mind that "Quality Score" measures emphasize the relation of your ad and its text to a "single specific theme," as the optimization guidelines inside Google AdWords suggests.

♦ Set up competing contextual ads on a couple of different search engines to see which perform better for you.

♦ Remember to time your testing carefully. It is usually not a good idea to conduct testing of different ad campaigns during the holiday shopping season or even during months when major holidays, such as the July 4th weekend, occur. The results could easily be skewed and not indicative of "normal" behavior in a more standard timeframe.

♦ Because this is still a relatively new process, be sure to seek the assistance of your advertising account representative if you are at all unsure about setting up campaigns in a way that will bring the best results. Likewise, if you are unhappy with the results of a contextual ad campaign you have run, go through the data with your search engine consultant or account manager and ask them to explain what didn't work properly, and why. Information gleaned from these sources can help in optimizing your website pages themselves for better ranking in organic results, by helping you learn in what ways content is of primary interest to today's search engines.

♦ If your funds are low, consider giving contextual advertising a try, because the cost per click is normally quite a bit lower than pay-per-click search. You may receive enough conversions to justify the campaign, and at the very least you will have gained some experience with the concept and techniques.

♦ Remember that there is a difference between the pay-per-click contextual search engines and websites that have contextual networks that you can advertise on. For example, Google and Yahoo! are search engines; Clicksor and Quigo are not. The latter rely on their network of publishers for placement of your contextual ads and thus require close attention to ensure that your ad is showing up in the kind of content that has the greatest potential of bringing you conversions— informational sites and review sites.

♦ Even though the non-search-engine contextual ad providers, such as Clicksor and Quigo, do not have the publisher base that the giant search engines have, they can provide a cheaper method of conducting a contextual ad campaign, and in an environment that many find easier to manage and track. The same is true of the smaller search engine's programs, such as those offered by Seevast (Kanoodle). However, keep in mind that the quality of clicks with those networks might be somewhat lower, as the best publishers tend to gravitate to the "big boys," who tend to pay more.

♦ Contextual advertising works best for advertisers who are most interested in increasing their number of impressions and their level of reach into the Internet marketplace. Because the ads show up without the visitor actively searching for sales information, they can be very useful in increasing your presence on the Internet in a less sales-driven fashion, which appeals to some more targeted results.

♦ With both PPC search and content, tracking is the key to success. Without knowing what is working and what is not—which keywords are converting or at least resulting in impressions—your ad dollars are being wasted. Take the time to investigate and analyze the data from any ad campaign.

♦ Remain aware that non-search-engine contextual ad providers tend to offer bidding based on vertical channels or categories such as travel, hotels, computers, etc.

Up until the move by Google to making "content" the ultimate test of relevancy, content advertising was a choice and chance that many website owners did not want to take. Aside from the impetus of quality content and relevance in every aspect of your website and your advertising campaigns, this past year has witnessed the maturation of the contextual ad market. It can be a very strong means of increasing your market reach across different types of websites you might otherwise never be able to penetrate.

After all, if you wanted to advertise in an offline version of a magazine, the cost of a full-page ad would be thousands of dollars and you would not be guaranteed placement next to relevant content. Online contextual ads are, by their very nature, placed within extremely relevant content and can cost pennies per click, for a total ad campaign cost that is a fraction of the offline version.

This discussion of relevance of content and context in online advertising logically leads to our next topics—the value of behavioral targeting and the concept of branding online. Like context advertising itself, these methods are relatively new and sometimes extremely controversial, but related to contextual advertising in that all have a similar goal—increasing the visibility of a business online.

Chapter 8 - Branding and Behavioral Targeting in Pay-Per-Click Advertising

One goal of advertising is to increase the positive perception that a customer has of the company from which they purchase products. If enough people know a company's name and what it stands for, a product (or the company itself) may reach the position where it is generally considered a brand name in a specific marketplace. A large part of branding depends upon repeat buyers, which marketers have attempted to reach via behavioral targeting in one form or another since humans made their first commercial transactions. Both branding and behavioral targeting have moved into the commercial side of the Internet, but with changes and levels of involvement different from other media.

Many advertisers believe that only large corporations (such as Microsoft, Nike, Wal-Mart, Coca-Cola, and so on) have the opportunity to become brand-name advertisers. But small-to-medium-sized businesses can also become involved in branding their product with the expectation of success, especially in the online world.

Why would this be the case? In a word—cost. Advertising online via pay-per-click search engines is vastly cheaper than advertising in the offline world, yet research shows that the online world reaches, and is used by, a significant proportion of consumers. A factor intimately intertwined with the notion of branding a product is the ability to reach the target audience in the most efficient means possible via behavioral targeting.

It's also interesting to note that, according to an estimate by Piper Jaffray released in November 2006 ("The New eCommerce Decade: The Age of Micro Targeting"), the average cost of acquiring a customer on the Internet is approximately $8.50, while Yellow Pages ads cost $20 per customer, offline display ads cost $50, email

> Online advertising is considered one of the most effective means of marketing a business, and it has the lowest per-sale cost.

marketing cost $60, and direct mail can go as high as $70. In other words, it's not just cheaper, but it is more effective. Granted, this data varies from one industry to another, but it does portray the proportionate breakdown between different advertising techniques.

With all the components of search covered in this book coming together (pay-per-click advertising, local search for PPC ads, contextual search ads, etc.), and demographics showing the most-likely-to-buy consumer as one who is also highly interested in the Internet, now is the time to use these tools and options to identify your target market and build a brand identity for yourself in that niche market—no matter how small your company or online presence is.

Of course, the prime driver for branding your product or company is repeat buyers. Without the same people buying your products repeatedly, thus becoming familiar with and valuing your products, it is difficult to obtain the sales or the increasingly valuable "word of mouth" factor needed to achieve notoriety online. Throughout 2005, behavioral targeting moved into online commerce as a means, not just of making initial sales, but of encouraging repeat buyers. We'll discuss the concept of behavioral targeting and how it's being practiced online later in this chapter.

For now, if you are successful at branding your product or company, you have, in effect, differentiated it from any other company selling the same product or service. Consumers view branded products as superior because they equate a higher value to them over the same product from a different company. In fact, the further you can remove your branded product from its competitors in terms of identity via name, packaging, advertising approach, or any number of other factors, the less likely it is that a consumer will purchase a substitute product instead of yours.

Therefore, if you wish to enter into branding online, you must focus on more than converting a visitor to a buyer—you must also get your company's message and values through to prospects and clients. The goal is to give visitors such a positive impression of your company that they will remember and mention your name as a possible source for others who are seeking the same product.

Methods PPC Advertisers Can Use to Brand Products

There are many approaches for increasing brand awareness of your company via pay per click. However, you must actively work to brand your product. Remember that you are trying to some extent to be in the same league as commercial giants such as Nike, whose trademark "swoosh" graphic immediately brings the word "Nike" to mind for almost any consumer interested in quality athletic footwear.

One good way to test the waters to see if you can make branding work in your pay-per-click advertising is to set up a separate ad campaign with branding as its ultimate goal.

This is not necessarily going to be an easy process, given that to some extent you are prevented by the search engines from using precisely the type of terminology that tends to build brand awareness. Wording such as "the world's best" or "number one in the United States" in a PPC ad description is quite often banned. Therefore, you must craft your ad so that the description includes, at the very least, the name of your company (prominently displayed). The addition of a logo (if allowed) is also a good idea. At this point, only a few pay-per-click search engines allow you to include a logo in ads.

There is still a fair amount of discussion about whether or not a unique selling point (USP) is a significant factor in helping to brand online. USP is certainly important for differentiating yourself from your competitors, and some analysts claim it is essential to draw visitors to your website by stating in your ad's description area that you offer something that no one else does.

Other analysts, however, think that a unique selling point is not critical to branding, because consumers are looking for an overall satisfactory consumer experience, not just being thrilled by the fact that you are the only company that gives away a free magazine subscription with every order over $100.

A study from 2004 by Millward Brown using 600 researchers in 16 countries asked the rather extreme question of, "Which company's brand name would you be willing to have tattooed on your body?" Although the first three answers are not too surprising (Harley Davidson, Disney, and Coca-Cola), the surprise fourth finisher was Google (at 6.6%, just one percent lower than Coca-Cola).

Given that there are other online markets as large and prominent as Google (e.g., Yahoo!, AOL, Netscape, eBay, Hotmail), the researchers speculate that people included Google in the list because they felt that Google, of all online entities, has been the most responsive to customer needs. Further, it has been the most open to revealing future plans via beta versions of a number of imaginative tools.

Even though the study is a couple of years old, it reiterates something that can't be emphasized enough—customer service is key, especially online, where your potential customer cannot visit your location in person and must rely on what you reveal of yourselves to them. Google was perceived as being very open with consumers—their goals, their works in progress, their plans to go public—well before they were required to. All of this worked to their favor and increased their brand awareness beyond the Google partner network.

Experimenting With Branding Online

If you pursue branding online, you need to realize that you may be at odds with the search engines in terms of your ultimate goal. You, as the advertiser, want the visitor to spend as much time as possible on your website, while the search engine is, to a significant degree, always interested in getting as many people to click on ads as possible to increase their revenue, thus leading to their wanting visitors to leave sites quickly and move on to another.

As a rule, a branding campaign is going to be more costly than a regular PPC campaign, because you will need to include many more generic keywords in your campaign than you might have otherwise, and having more generic keywords is generally more costly.

Because the key factor in branding is a high degree of awareness of your product, you need to capture as many site visitors as possible. Thus, you want to select the generic keywords that people who are just beginning the buying cycle will plug into the search box. In addition, you must bid high enough on the keywords to end up high in the list and have content that is considered "relevant" enough to satisfy the content network (and to some degree the search network) or your ads will not be active. Keep in mind that you do not have to pay for these sometimes expensive keywords unless someone actually clicks on the ad.

Research reported in February 2005 by DoubleClick and comScore, who tracked 1.5 million consumers who had purchased online, revealed how important generic keywords are if you are pursuing a branding strategy.

The results of their study showed that, generally speaking, the buying cycle falls within a 12-week period. During that time, it is usually not until the final stage, when the decision to purchase has been made, that searchers use specific keywords that include company names and other branding-related terms.

Even during the last week of the buying cycle, almost one-fifth of the searches were still generic in nature. This implies that branding opportunities can exist even at this late stage, and that a small business could be the choice over an already-known brand name. If this happens often enough, you could see the beginning of your own branding.

If you have kept your company's name and identifying characteristics in the forefront over the entire buying cycle of an individual consumer, comScore believes that you have a relatively good chance of not only converting that customer to a purchaser, but more importantly, of increasing your brand awareness to that consumer.

It is also important to plan your strategy well and to decide in advance all the details of how you want your brand to be perceived. What are the key factors you want to portray? These need not necessarily be unique selling points, but are aspects that consumers seek and expect, and that will encourage them to become repeat buyers. Examples include being open 24/7, having a wide selection of goods, low shipping costs, and so on.

When brainstorming, consider the companies that you think of as brand names and then come up with a list of the properties that made them, and continues to make them, a name that is instantly associated with a product. After you have identified those items, figure out if you can duplicate similar aspects in your products.

Equally important to your ad campaign is ensuring that your website is clear, clean, and very intuitive for a potential visitor to use. Reassess your web design and make sure there are no inconsistencies in your content, particularly centering on purchasing requirements or the purchasing process itself.

Be sure to include testimonials, especially if you have a customer who is already well known, because some of their own branding will rub off on your site (the user will think, "if 'X' company uses these people, then they must be good").

Remember that ad impressions from a regular PPC campaign or a contextual advertising ad campaign can go a long way toward helping brand your products. Repeated exposure on content-based sites, and impressions gained through organic search results, will put your ads in front of the consumer repeatedly. Because many studies have shown it is rare for a single exposure to an ad to result in a purchase, the more times your ads are seen by potential customers, the more likely you are to convert them into buyers.

There are some specific concerns to keep in mind if you do set up a branding campaign:

- ◆ A branding campaign is usually long-term, and can yield a lower return than a campaign developed for direct response. For one thing, the majority of online purchases go through a sales cycle that averages 12 weeks. During this time, the consumer researches the product, researches some potential sellers, mulls the situation over for a while, and then decides from whom to purchase. And as stated previously, the generic keywords that are essential to branding tend to be much more expensive than the "niche" keywords that may be part of your PPC search advertising campaigns.

- ◆ Monitor your branding campaign to ensure that the number of impressions without clickthroughs does not wind up disabling your search terms. Otherwise, it may take you some time to recover your traditional PPC ad campaign once your experiment with branding is over.

- ◆ Continually rethink the campaign, tweaking keywords where necessary and varying your ads ever so slightly if your initial results don't bear fruit or if you see that a slightly different approach works better.

- ◆ Consider setting up a very short mini-poll on your thank-you page (or on an appropriate page for earlier in the buying cycle) asking why consumers made a purchase, whether or not your efforts met their expectations, and how you could improve the experience for them. A good customer experience is vital to branding, not just in the quality of your product, but in the interest you show in your consumers. You may receive some insightful comments in return, and the poll serves as a further reminder of the company from which they have just purchased a product.

A study conducted by AdKnowledge in late summer of 2003 found that conversions that occur long after the initial clickthrough to the PPC ad were on the rise. In fact, around 44% of total conversions in the study were repeat conversions, indicating that

> Approximately half of all online orders come from repeat visitors, not first-time users.

building customer loyalty (and eventually branding) is not only possible on the Internet, but perhaps a larger player than currently realized.

Another study undertaken in the same time period revealed that the Top 50 most visited sites (resulting from online advertising) were not the largest US corporations, but rather companies such as Amazon.com, eBay.com, eToy.com, and so on. A November 2006 study by ZDNet revealed that although the first search term used at the Top 10 shopping sites such as Amazon and eBay are generic category terms (e.g., furniture, shoes), the second search term entered is a brand name (e.g., Barbie, Lego, Air Force Ones).

Part of the success of a site such as Amazon is that they also offer items that someone coming to buy books might be interested in. This includes such things as music, movies, children's toys, and a variety of other products they have carefully researched and identified as being of interest to book purchasers.

Every time you look at the details of a book, you will also find a list of other books or products that people, like you, looked at in more detail while on the Amazon site. All of this is designed to keep the visitor on the site as long as possible, and perhaps tempt them to place more items in their shopping cart than they originally came prepared to purchase.

If the consumer is happy with the related items they have decided to purchase, it's a certainty that they will come back to Amazon the next time they are in the market for a book—and the branding process has begun.

Of course, Amazon has already branded itself online, precisely through such methods. It evolved from a simple bookstore many years ago to a complex site where you can purchase any number of related products. You will also be exposed to unrelated products that Amazon has found make good impulse buys.

The example of Amazon leads to a very important consideration. How can you tell if your branding approach is working? In short, what indications should you look for to see if the ad campaign you are running is working and actually increasing your brand recognition?

Not surprisingly perhaps, the types of statistics that you need to analyze most closely are quite different from those in PPC search ads. They are, in fact, closer to the type of statistics one looks at to evaluate contextual advertising, because both branding and contextual advertising share one thing in common—they depend upon people repeatedly seeing your ad.

Therefore, the key analytics to track after you have let your branding campaign run through at least one complete buying cycle (about 12 weeks, plus tacking on a week or two on either end if you can afford to) are:

- ◆ **Traffic**—keep a close eye on the traffic to your site during your branding campaign. Not only does this tell you how many people are visiting your site, so that you can compare those statistics with a similar PPC search engine ad campaign, it will help you ensure all your keywords are active for search and have not been disabled due to a clickthrough rate below the search engine's default percentage or a "quality score" type of disabling.

- ◆ **Average Position (ranking)**—a study conducted by the Interactive Advertising Bureau in mid-2004 strongly indicated that top ranking in search results increased brand awareness by about 27%. Top positions tend to reach partner networks more readily as well, thereby increasing the number of people who will see them.

- ◆ **Impressions**—this analytic is, of course, the main key to branding. Just as with offline advertising, your goal is to get as many "eyeballs" on the page as possible, as marketing people term it. Online, this obviously means getting as many people as possible to see your ad, even if they do not take any further action.

  The repeated viewing of your ad will, over time, increase your chances of achieving some success in branding your product or your company name.

After all, in the course of about seven years, Google went from a two-person start-up in a dorm room at Stanford University to a company known worldwide as the top search engine.

If you are sufficiently motivated, manage to find the finances needed to carry on a long-term branding campaign, work hard at pleasing the customer, and can find a unique presence (even if you offer the same product or service as others), you may become the next "Google" or "Amazon."

Although it may seem impossible to break through that invisible barrier as a small business, there are cases that show it can be done.

Additional Tips on Branding Online

There is no doubt about it—branding and the possibility of success versus the cost involved is a very controversial topic. It is not a cheap option, nor is it foolproof. One should enter into such a venture knowing that initial results will be slow in coming and that you may never reach your ultimate goal. However, you may be able to increase the number of repeat customers along the way and move a little closer to that goal.

Here are a few final tips to help you if you decide to undertake a branding advertising campaign on a PPC search engine:

♦ **Keywords**—although the general approach is to bid on generic keywords, do not overlook including keywords of any trademarked products/services you may have. If the product/service is not officially trademarked, but is unique to your offerings, also add keywords for those items to your branding campaign. These keywords will cost very little, since they are trademarked and/or unique to your particular company, and one of these terms may be what stuck in the mind of a previous buyer or visitor who can't remember your URL or your company name. Do consider the legal implications of using keywords that are the names of products not yet trademarked if you decide to include them.

♦ **ROI**—in a branding ad campaign, Return on Investment (ROI) is not the only key analytic to worry about. The goal of a branding campaign is not just to sell products right away (although that is also considered), but rather to imprint your company's name and/or products on the visitor's mind in order to prompt future visits. Expect the ROI on a branding campaign to be smaller at first, so you won't be disappointed if it turns out that way, as it almost invariably will.

♦ **Experimentation**—keep in mind that a branding ad campaign, especially when you first dip your toes in the water, is an experiment. Don't expect great results from the beginning, but carefully analyze and compare the number of impressions and amount of traffic between this campaign and a regular PPC ad campaign. A comparison will not be easy, since the keywords used in either case will not be the same, but enough data should be available to give you a rough idea about whether or not you want to invest more money and time in more branding approaches.

♦ **Competition**—if you run an organic search on "soft drinks," you will not find websites for the top brand names coming up in the first pages of a search result. Instead, you will typically see informational sites talking about soft drinks. The large companies, such as Coca-Cola and PepsiCo, don't need to be top ranked online because they already have well-established brand names offline. Therefore, your competition for what may be considered a highly relevant generic keyword may not be other companies selling soft drinks, but contextual websites. There are significant opportunities available to help you brand your particular soft drink in such an environment.

♦ **Contextual Advertising and Branding**—if a search for a generic product is more likely to turn up informational websites rather than the large brand names that control the marketplace, consider using contextual ads within those sites as a means of indirectly branding your product.

Behavioral Targeting

Behavioral targeting is a cousin to branding as far as online advertising is concerned, in that both depend upon feedback about those who purchase products and action upon that feedback in order to succeed.

Behavioral targeting is simply the targeting of ad material to a certain audience based on past behavior. It also encompasses the targeting of ads based on demographics such as age, gender, income, culture, language, etc.

Still in relative infancy in online use, behavioral targeting has been used in direct-response advertising and other media for many years. TV shows, for example, are almost always geared to a particular demographic and the advertising that accompanies the program is likewise selected for the likelihood of appealing to that demographic. For example, cartoons are generally targeted towards children, and ads tend to be for toys, games, breakfast cereal, snacks, and the like.

Online, behavioral targeting has been slow in getting started. One of the major concerns limiting its growth is privacy. Although consumers have largely accepted and are willing to share personal information for offline commercial purposes, most people on the Internet want to believe that they are acting anonymously.

Most of the behavioral targeting currently practiced online is done by agencies on big-budget accounts, but for the average business owner, there are many ways to track a visitor through your website using third-party tracking software and/or analyzing your site's traffic logs. The smallest detail can be tracked—not just how a visitor moves around your website and which pages they spend time on, but even the website they go to after they leave yours.

Thus, you can track the "behavior" of a visitor on your website and deduce from that behavior a great deal of information about changes you should and should not make to your site or to your PPC ads.

By analyzing the movement of visitors through your site, you can revise the placement of products, so that those most often searched for are easy to access, associated accessories or related items are presented together with your main products, and even feed specific product information to those who have purchased from you in the past.

Much of the behavioral targeting of ads online is carried out in vertical search, where visitors choose a category before (or just after) beginning their search. Therefore, an advertiser has already jumped the first hurdle—the visitor is interested in, for example, electronics—and so you have already pre-qualified your visitors as interested in what you have to offer.

It currently works better in some categories more so than others—automotive, travel, and electronics are three definite leaders in succeeding in behavioral targeting. To a large degree, this is because research, and common sense, tells a business owner what kind of person is most likely to be in the demographic of those looking to buy a car—they are more likely to be male, probably in their 20s and 30s, etc.

What do you do if you either don't want to advertise on vertical search engines or your product or service doesn't easily fit into one of those niches? You can still take advantage of behavioral targeting, even though it is relatively under-exploited as a marketing technique online at this time.

The major search engines are already moving into the area of behavioral targeting. If you use the AdWords program, for example, Google Analytics will help you segment your traffic so that you can determine the type of people who are clicking on your PPC ads—where they are from, what time of day or day of the week your ads are most successful, and other factors.

When setting up your ad campaigns, you can segment visitors so that anyone who visits a particular page is tracked as a "technology" user, for example. By tracking the aggregate behavior of all those tagged as belonging to that segment, you can fine tune your ad campaigns and make changes to your website to better target that audience.

Google also collects a lot of information concerning the behavior of those who use the search engine through Google Desktop and the Google Toolbar, in addition to more basic methods. Although Google has yet to officially come out with a "behavioral targeting" package for advertisers, much of the move towards contextually relevant results is intertwined with behaviors online.

Yahoo! Search Marketing already sells its category-based ads using behavioral targeting. They currently have about 400 categories that they classify visitors into depending upon their behavior online on the Yahoo! site itself, not on the paid search results. Yahoo! segments searchers into two streams—Engagers (who have recently shown interest in a product category) and Shoppers (whose online behavior indicates more activity, which may indicate they are further in the buying cycle). Advertisers who are trying to build brand recognition are encouraged to aim for the Engagers, while those running ads with special offers and direct response advertisers are encouraged to focus on the Shoppers.

Microsoft adCenter is in the midst of integrating behavioral targeting into its process in a huge way. Microsoft has an advantage because they collect a fair amount of personal demographic information from millions of users via registration forms for Microsoft products and subscriber forms for Windows Live services and other ventures. This is how they describe the current state of their behavioral targeting endeavor:

"We incorporated extensive client and industry input to construct each specific behavioral segment. In accordance with our privacy statement, we blend the information that customers offer to us, such as their age and gender, with search and browse histories from MSN and Windows Live. We customize the timeframe we analyze depending on the typical purchase cycle (longer for cars, shorter for movie watchers). We then use advanced technologies from our adCenter Labs to develop an innovative matchmaking service to deliver advertiser's messages.

As a simple example, a customer who's been researching new cars on MSN Autos and searching for Kelly Blue Book prices on Windows Live Search is likely in the market for a new car. When this customer visits MSN, we would deliver ads relevant to someone shopping for a new car."

(Microsoft's Meera Bhatia, group product planner—from an interview by Anna Papadopoulous on November 8, 2006)

As behavioral targeting in search engine advertising becomes more sophisticated and widespread, concerns about privacy will be expressed and will have to be addressed by search engines to the satisfaction of the average user. Advertisers already have issues with users deleting cookies used to track their behavior while on-site and during return visits.

Even some burgeoning technologies such as Ajax (which moves the presentation of numerous pages of product information to the user's computer all at once, instead of making separate calls to each page) will affect how the concept of a "page view" is defined, likely making it more difficult to track.

In the quest to make search and website advertising more and more relevant and create a "good user experience," all kinds of issues and concerns will come into play. Branding and behavioral targeting of advertising are two goals every business will pursue to some extent, no matter the size of the business, in order to succeed online.

So far, we've considered a number of types of pay-per-click advertising available and some different approaches that may help extend the reach of your product and your company. As yet, we haven't explored the opposite notion—how a small business (perhaps one that does not even have a website) can gain a share of the increasing number of consumers making purchases via online methods or contacts.

The next chapter discusses the explosive growth of an answer to this dilemma—local search—an approach that works even (some might say "especially") for companies that do not have a website!

Chapter 9 - Local Pay-Per-Click Advertising

What Is Local PPC Advertising and Why Should You Consider It?

Local targeting, which allows an advertiser to target PPC ad campaigns to the local market, is a trend that matured significantly through 2006 and has become an integral part of pay-per-click advertising.

Website developers have gradually come to realize that many people research products and services online, but then buy them at a local outlet. This fact affects all kinds of businesses. This behavior has been substantiated by many reliable research reports over the past few years; a June 2006 report by The Kelsey Group found that "43% of search engine users are seeking a local merchant to buy something offline .... and 54% of search users have substituted Internet/search for the phone book, mostly for specific local lookups." Statistics such as these lead to the conclusion that the conversion rate of visitors into buyers may be higher if a PPC ad is targeted to the visitor's geographic region.

On the other side of the coin, local businesses may be reluctant to place marketing money into a website, much less a pay-per-click campaign, because they know the majority of the visitors to their website are probably located

> 59% of merchants surveyed by WebAdvantage said that they would use PPC ads, if they could target their local market.

too far away to purchase from them. Despite the many studies proving otherwise, some still choose to believe that the average consumer does not feel comfortable ordering merchandise online. Still, research conducted by WebAdvantage found that 59% of merchants they surveyed would use PPC ads online if they could target their local market.

The History of Local Search on the Internet

Some websites have offered a local search component since the late 1990s, but these components are mainly confined to comparison shopping sites and directory-style sites. Their efforts have not always matched the needs of the marketplace, but they reaped the benefit of realizing the importance of local search before most other search engines did.

More recently, the growing complexity of local search makes it difficult to generalize. Local search has grown to include geo-targeted searches and mapped search from search engines, directory or category-based shopping sites and other vertical directory markets, and the expanding online presence of internet yellow pages (IYPs) and their integration into search engines.

The advertising revenues associated with the overall sector of local search (which includes not just local Internet search, but also IYP properties and mobile directory-based search) may be worth as much as $31.1 billion globally by 2010, up from $15.7 billion in 2005, according to research from The Kelsey Group in a November 2006 report.

Most importantly, however, what has not changed is evidence of the increasing efficacy of using local search in online advertising campaigns. A March 2006 study by comScore (using the search behavior of 83 million Americans in 552 million searches using one or more of 24 leading search engines) showed that 25% of searchers ultimately purchased an item related to their search query.

Even more interesting, 37% of those purchasing an item did so online, while 63% purchased offline at a local store. The cycle of "research online and buy offline" still is the most likely pattern. This means different things to different businesses. It emphasizes the need for brick-and-mortar outlets to move advertising dollars online to capture the part of the market that is researching online but wishing to buy locally. To those already online, adjustments to ad campaigns may bring some of that local market online, or it can be diverted to their brick-and-mortar outlets with some modifications in their sales process.

Two key points from the research deserve repeating here:

♦ One-fourth of all search queries ultimately resulted in a purchase (whether it be offline or online).

♦ Almost two-thirds of those shopping online ultimately purchase from a local store.

Research released in September 2006 by comScore Networks showed that 63% of US Internet users (an estimated 109 million persons), performed a local search in July, which is a 43% increase over July of 2005. The total number of local searches in July was in the neighborhood of 849 million.

How does this all fit with pay-per-click advertising? Given the growing influence of local search over the past couple of years, many search engines have at the very least introduced a geo-targeting option into their PPC programs, while others have added a local search component to the engine itself.

Encouraging this trend is evidence such as that presented in a June 2006 report from The Kelsey Group that determined:

• 35% of online shoppers said they were "loyal" to one search engine

• 53% said that they used two or three search engines

- 10% indicated they used four or more search engines regularly.

Clearly, if a search engine can capture the attention of an individual browser and provide them with the local search experience that brings them what they want, when they want, and in a form they find easy to process, they may prove to be quite loyal to that particular engine. Not such a surprising find, as it parallels the individual's experience with search overall, but to businesses online, this parallel translates directly into increased ROI from advertising on specific search engines.

To small businesses in particular, the ability to run a local search is a huge development. This finally gives you the opportunity to persuade Internet customers who like to buy locally to choose **your** business over the store three blocks away, without even having to interact with them.

Many businesses have become disillusioned with organic search results. They have found that PPC is a reliable option for their ad dollars, and adding the local touch is the icing on the cake. Local PPC search is definitely worth investigating and experimenting with to see if it can help you increase your ROI by converting more of the visitors to your website into buyers (and hopefully repeat buyers).

Let's take a look at where the major PPC search engines currently sit in terms of local PPC advertising and local search in general. Vertical search engines/directories and internet yellow pages, which usually charge a "per listing" cost versus a pay-per-click charge, are more successful in the local ad market, but the major search engines offering PPC are making strides to improve their market share.

Local PPC Search Engines

Major PPC search engines began adding local search to their programs in 2005. The two largest, Google and Yahoo!, added the component early in 2004, but have made major changes to their offerings since then. Microsoft reinvented its complete advertising program , with local search included, throughout the last half of 2006. Another search engine, Interchange, reinvested itself as Local.com and has chosen to concentrate on local advertising.

Other search engines have made smaller changes, mostly in the form of offering some degree of geo-targeting in their PPC offerings, so that an advertiser can choose to have their ads shown only in certain geographic markets. Others have allied themselves with providers of local contact information (particularly yellow page properties), but the advertising options rarely include the pay-per-click model.

One advertising model that shows promise, but has proven to be somewhat difficult to put into practice, is pay-per-call advertising. Obviously, there are logistical considerations for a business that buys online advertising that, once clicked by a searcher, will cause their telephone to ring. If the connection is made, the strength of a voice-to-voice sales pitch to someone who has already shown interest in your product can be very compelling, but issues such as 24-hour coverage of phone calls, busy signals, trained staff at the phones, and the like have proved problematic. The move of advertising to the mobile platform may mitigate these issues or, at the very least, force businesses to deal with the consequences of local search involving the phone and mobile phone market.

For the rest of this chapter, let's concentrate on the options for pay-per-click advertising offered by four leading local search providers.

Google AdWords

Local search has been fully integrated into the Google product, moving from beta to mainstream in 2006. Local sponsored results (PPC ads) are in the usual placement area along the right side of the page.

The search engine looks at a searcher's query phrase for several factors before choosing which ads to display. The searcher's Google domain location is key—for example, if a searcher is using the German domain, they are assumed to be interested in information from that domain, even if their IP address indicates they are located in Japan. If an actual region or city (or zip code) is entered, the same logic applies. The IP address is usually only used by itself if no other information regarding locale is provided in the search query.

If you want to use local search (or geo-targeting) in your PPC ad campaign, advertisers have powerful options in deciding how large to cast the net. They can concentrate on regions and cities if their market extends that far, or can map out a radius or define a specific area to target your ads more precisely.

If you make your local ad area too small, however, you will not only receive much less traffic than you might have expected, but your impression rate may drop below acceptable levels, particularly if your Quality Score is not up to par.

The key to overall improvement in Google Local throughout 2005 and 2006 was the integration of Google Maps into the product. Any advertiser can place a free business ad that will appear on Google Maps when a searcher either uses Google Maps or chooses "Maps" after an organic search focusing on local businesses.

A map of the area you have targeted (5 mile radius, for example) comes up along with the local listings, each with a letter assigned to them that matches a small balloon on the map, indicating the location on a street grid. The user can dynamically change the focus of the search and add a satellite view to the regular map if they wish.

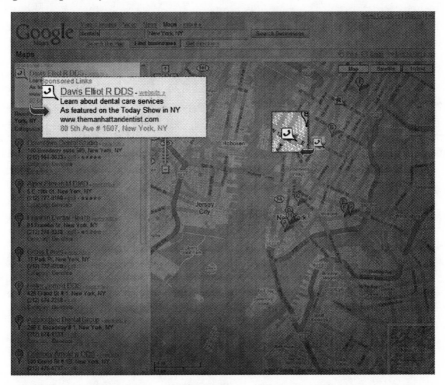

Figure 9.1 – A quick search for "dentists" in New York produced this results page.

The listing for an individual local business includes the name, phone number, address of the business, and a URL (if the location has a website). A "Directions" link will provide driving directions once the user enters their starting (and end) point. The searcher can also read any reviews of the business that have been written by others, as well as access a results page for a search on the business itself.

If you are interested in participating in Google Local through the AdWords program, setting up the parameters is a fairly easy process. Different campaigns can be set to different location variables (e.g., one ad targeted to the city as a whole and another targeted to searches within a certain distance from your location). Keep in mind that the smaller you make your search radius in your ad, the less traffic you are likely to receive, as your ad will only show up if someone specifies a location within your set region.

Although a September 2006 study by comScore showed that Google sites (note the plural) garnered 29.8% of local searches in the US in July of that year, further details of the study reveal its limitations. For example, those searching in their own locale were primarily searching for dining information or other entertainment-related locations (59%), followed by 52% searching for an actual business address or phone, and 41% searching for specific services in their location (including lawyers, dry cleaners and car rentals).

At this point, one problem with local search on Google is that to be shown the most important local information, the user must also click on the "Maps" option in addition to a local search query. Alternatively, they can click on the "Local Results for 'dentists near New York'" at the top of the organic listing SERPs to access the mapped information, but this option is not particularly user friendly for the average searcher.

Still, Google is increasingly integrating small businesses. A recent decision to provide a free webpage to businesses that do not have a website (or wish not to provide one) may encourage local businesses to advertise using Google.

In the end, however, the proven success of other search engines (many of which use a vertical category-type of interface) in driving local search may provide the impetus for Google to make its local search option more intuitive.

Yahoo! Search Marketing

The Yahoo! local offering for advertisers is similar to that found at Google, although Yahoo! adds extra value in its placement of ads within vertical categories and offers a more robust customer experience.

Yahoo! also offers a free basic local listing of contact information, website and email, hours, payment methods, products and service offered, and a business category. For $10 per month, you can add a logo, photos, more detail and placement in five categories, as well as two links to special offers.

The Geo-Targeting Sponsored Search program works much like the Google program, with the tie-in between local search and mapping. If a searcher enters a local parameter in the search box, sponsored results are returned along the top and side of the results page, if any PPC ads are available for that location. If, however, a user accesses the "Local" option on the main query box page, they are prompted for a product/service type and a zip code or city.

The organic SERP listings that follow can be sorted by price, rating, name, or distance from their current location (as Yahoo! has determined it). Searchers can also click to get a map or a phone connection, rather than clicking on the company name.

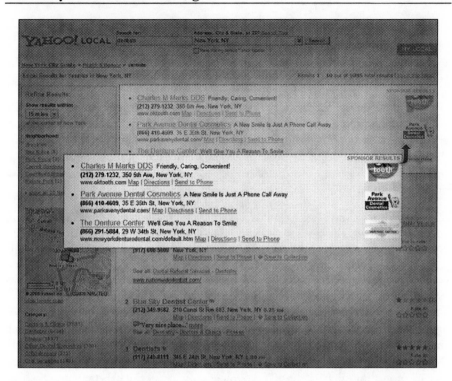

Figure 9.2 – A search for "dentists" in New York on Yahoo! produced this results page.

When a user clicks on your PPC ad, they are taken to an interim page called the Locator Page, which has a map to your business, customized information about your business, a link to get driving directions (a small map is shown by default), and the URL of your website. Users can also write a review of your business on this page or look at the other linked listings displayed. Various services near your business, such as public transportation, ATM machines, and hotels, are also shown.

This interim page allows the advertiser to provide a lot of information to potential clients without requiring them to visit the website. More importantly, perhaps, it allows advertisers who do not have websites to participate, since a URL is not required to participate in the program.

All of the relevant information can be included on this page and, in fact, because the main results page includes a link to contact the business via a text message sent to a phone, businesses without a website can also easily take advantage of the service.

Alternatively, by clicking on the "Dentists Near New York – Local Results" item located just under the sponsored results, the user will be taken to Yahoo!

Local, for a map of the area with the search results identified by letters. However, the resulting map is not very attractive, with results piled on top of each other. The user needs to zoom in or adjust the view in order to see the results in any usable fashion.

Another interesting feature is as you hover over the listings on the map, the map zooms in and a small popup appears identifying the business, its address, and phone number. Unfortunately, this map obscures the search listings while displayed. Alternatively, if you click on a number in the map itself, you go directly to the business locator page. If you wish to visit the website, another click is necessary.

The signup process is fairly intuitive and similar to Google. If you are located, or wish to target consumers, outside of the US or Canada, you will need to contact Yahoo! directly for assistance in setting up your geo-targeting campaign.

Yahoo! is poised to unveil its new ad platform, code-named Panama, and has begun migrating advertisers over, with expectations of completion early in 2007. Preliminary information about the local advertising option is that it has been significantly improved, particularly in the ability to target your campaign much more precisely (down to the city and Designated Market Area or DMA level). When setting up an account, the geo-targeting decision is among the first to be made, indicating that Yahoo! recognizes the power local targeting has to maximize results.

Microsoft Live (previously MSN) - adCenter

Microsoft made huge strides in PPC advertising in general throughout 2006. The development of their adCenter site and the switch over to the "Live" sites is still underway, but should prove to be a strong challenger to Google and Yahoo!

In terms of local search, Microsoft Local Live has much the same capabilities and architectural setup as Google and Yahoo! Organic search results for a search within a city bring up a link to local results at the top of the search engine results page (called "top local listings for …"). At this point, targeting by zip code, state, or DMA is not available.

Clicking on the link takes you to a setup with tagged results on a map and ads for each entry. The sponsored local ads at the top of this page are identified as being supplied by SuperPages. If you do not identify the location of your search, your IP address will be used to provide local listings. International targeting is limited to those searching using a country-specific Microsoft domain – for example, if you target France, your ads will only be shown to people using the French Microsoft domain and having an IP address located in France.

Microsoft's current advantage is in their 3-D-capable version of mapping, Virtual Earth. A user can adjust the angle at which they view satellite imagery, resulting in a more visually appealing approach of orienting oneself at street level or at a 45-degree angle, in addition to the top-down view offered by Google Earth. Unfortunately, coverage of areas outside of the US is incomplete at closer levels of magnification.

To add geographic targeting to your Microsoft Live campaigns, however, be prepared to pay an incremental bid amount, in addition to your PPC bid, for what is considered an "extra" service.

Overall, the Microsoft offering is not quite as flexible as Google or Yahoo!, but the local search options for users are much more robust. As Microsoft's offering becomes more competitive in terms of an advertiser's needs, the visual power of Virtual Earth will become an even greater advantage.

Local.com (formerly Interchange)

Local.com challenges the "Big 3" search engines with a site totally devoted to local search. The search engine debuted in 2005, supplementing the parent company's offerings via its local search and advertising platform (Local Direct™), which combined Interchange's paid-search platform with a robust local business database, and the company's proprietary Keyword DNA™ technology, to create a comprehensive local-search solution.

Local.com offers a free basic listing to all businesses, in addition to its PPC ad product. PPC ads are based on an auction model and are placed on SERPs depending upon keyword and category. They also offer a "Local Featured Sponsor" option that guarantees your ad will be placed above organic results and allows you to target by geographic region in addition to keywords. Their other product, "LocalPromote" ties your ad to the mapping section, while a premium option will also give you a "featured sponsor" position on the search engine. LocalPromote business listings are distributed outside of the Local.com network to Google Local, Yahoo! Local, SuperPages.com, Switchboard.com, among others and have a monthly fee associated with them.

With Local.com, the searcher enters a query term and location into the search box and the relevant businesses near the location appear on a results page. Sponsor links (which could link to Yahoo! or Google Local's map results page), and featured sponsors (with a link to the business website), are listed first, followed by "Local Results," which have even more sponsored links at the top.

In a search for "dentists" and "New York," one has to scroll down a fair way to even reach the organic results, as so many paid ads are shown at the top of the page. The organic results, however, can be sorted by relevance, distance or in alphabetical order. Each listing has options of accessing a map/directions or writing a review in addition to clicking through to the website.

Local.com's database has over 16 million business listings, but is limited to the United States in its coverage, using zip codes as its primary means of identification. A study by comScore in July 2006 shows monthly page views of 38 million and monthly searches close to 19 million.

The search engine's technology effectively bridges the gap between keyword search and category-based directory search, and enables directory publishers and website owners to enter the growing online local-search market, with the strength of the company's expansive networks and advanced technology at their disposal. Local.com is fast becoming a contender for placement among search engines offering PPC advertising, and their early integration of a mobile device platform (where the user can access Local.com on their mobile device and click to call a business directly) should help solidify that position.

Tips on Improving a Local PPC Campaign

For local search, the usual PPC tips such as ensuring that the landing page is one designed to encourage a sale need to be supplemented. A few suggestions are:

- Include as much local information (phone numbers, city name, etc.) as allowed in your local PPC ad, not just your URL.

- Become more familiar with the types of products/services that are best suited for local purchasing to ensure local search will really improve your ROI and not just add expense to your budget. Some types of products are more often purchased locally than others. For example, professional services (such as doctors, lawyers, and the like) usually do well with local search options, while products/services that consumers are used to purchasing online (such as CDs, movies, etc.) may not.

- Investigate the pay-per-call options that some PPC search engines are now offering, especially if you do not have a website. Wireless search has begun to infiltrate the online community and can be a useful means of integrating local search into paid ads if you do not have a website.

- Research before you decide which PPC local search engine to use. Try some searches on your own for products you would like to buy locally and see how well the results fit your search. This can help you judge potential results before you even sign up to try out a new service.

- Ask your PPC representative for assistance on how to make your ad more appealing to a local market.

- ♦ Remember that a search engine that only uses IP addresses as a means of tracking local users will not be as accurate as one that uses a geographic method to target them. Be sure you know which method of tracking is being used to deliver local results.

- ♦ Figure out what is unique about your product/service compared to the business five blocks away, and then include this information in your local ad to gain further advantage. Examples might include "open 24/7," a comment on low prices, or free delivery.

Above all, remember that once you have a local pay-per-click advertising campaign running, you must focus on competing against other businesses just like yours within the same local area (how wide depends on your search engine options and your ad budget). Therefore, make your local ad as unique and compelling as possible. You must offer something to set your business apart from your **local** competitors.

Internet Yellow Pages, City Guides, and Comparison Shopping Search Engines

Until very recently, paid advertising on Internet yellow page and/or city guide websites was not considered by most small-to-medium-sized businesses to be a viable choice. This was perhaps because of the cost versus estimated number of visitors, or because online advertisers did not think many users accessed citywide types of directories, or that they just used the review sections of online comparison shopping sites.

However, with a strong move toward producing much larger, more robust entities, Internet yellow pages (or IYPs) have become bigger players in the online advertising market. However, since most IYP advertising is not strictly pay per click in nature, they do not directly compete with established search engines and many have entered into agreements with search engines to integrate.

Internet yellow page companies, as they began to partner with online search engines whose databases ensure that up-to-date listings are quickly integrated into searches, soon realized that they could sell the equivalent of PPC ads inside their online yellow page sites, in addition to online traditional advertising.

Each side realizes the other's strengths—proven online customer reach and existing PPC programs in place on the search engines (for example, the name recognition of Google and its listing as the most popular search engine), and the yellow page companies' proven print reach and the increasing use of their online sites by potential customers.

Looking at a couple of examples, Verizon SuperPages.com has developed a complete PPC solution for advertisers based on research showing that 80% of those who use their website to locate a business contact an advertiser and 53% actually make a purchase. The package involves a minimum monthly spend of $15 in clicks and also offers assistance in setting up and maintaining an account for a monthly fee.

At the same time, they also have an agreement with Google to sell the AdWords program, acting as a middle person between small businesses who do not wish to set up their own PPC campaigns. Indeed, the situation appears to be leaning toward further consolidation and collaborating between the search engines and Internet yellow page and directory-style paid listings.

Shopping comparison sites including Shopzilla (BizRate), NexTag, and Shopping.com are also early adopters of this hybrid. The vertical search market is, indeed, the main place in which one would expect to find local search proliferating; however, as consumers become more sophisticated online, many choose to shop online, rather than look for a local merchant online, diluting the strength of these sites to move products to local businesses.

Conclusion

The partnerships that are continuing to form between PPC search engines and online phone directories are proving very interesting in their impact on PPC as a whole. The large online phone directories are continuing to pursue local online advertising strongly. They are contracting not just with the PPC search engines, but with online shopping sites and other directory-style sites.

For both PPC search engines and local businesses, it is key to remember that the point of a PPC ad is to make it unique enough that you do not receive a lot of clicks that do not convert to sales. Although Microsoft Live is catching up, so far only Google and Yahoo! offer a robust enough experience to suitably impress visitors with the advantages of using local search.

One of the key factors to keep in mind is that local search, partially because of its connection to Internet yellow page properties and partially because of search engines offering free "mini" sites, allows businesses without websites to participate and profit from the pay-per-click marketplace.

Because local search providers do not require that an advertiser have a website in order to compete for placement on local searches, a whole new avenue of advertising has opened up for businesses that want to benefit from online searches. It allows them to compete on a more level playing field with local competitors who have websites, and it allows them to reach the large percentage of online consumers who search the Internet for product information or to narrow their choices before purchasing locally.

The key is reaching those local businesses. Most are relatively small and few have enough experience with search engines to feel comfortable with starting an ad campaign from scratch. Yellow page properties are a comfortable fit for them—their usual salesperson comes around for their yellow page ad and offers them an online opportunity that is ready-made and requires no extra effort from them.

The search engines need to compete with the ease of this process if they wish to emerge as the winner in local search. Steps have been taken, but more needs to be done to ensure success in dominating paid search online for the local market. Certainly, the Google AdWords Starter Edition is a step in this direction, as is the "web page without a domain name" offer for local search.

Google has also taken a step towards leading the move online for small business with its very recent agreement with Intuit software to work the AdWords program into the workflow of their tax and business planning/record keeping software. This may prove to be the key needed to garner the business of many small companies, using the goodwill generally associated with the Intuit business brand.

Expect the battle between the main contenders in local PPC search to continue to heat up, particularly as the Yahoo! Panama platform becomes fully integrated. There are certain to be advancements in both Yahoo! and Microsoft offerings to counter the broad strokes that Google has undertaken to lure local business online in a simple and non-threatening manner.

Smaller search engines may also improve upon their current local products, which tend to be limited and seem almost experimental in nature. As with PPC in general, the larger engines still control the environment, but the chance is always there that with the right product, any market could open up to challenge them.

The next chapter begins our look at the specific details of the top search engines offering PPC programs, followed by a look at some smaller properties and some tools to help you with your PPC ad campaigns, before we turn to some of the trends we think will influence the next couple of years of PPC advertising.

Chapter 10 – Types of Pay-Per-Click Search Engines and Reviews

So far, we've discussed various means of advertising online using pay-per-click methods. Although a number of search engines have been mentioned along the way, we want to present you with a systematic analysis of the different types of search engines available and provide you with reviews to help you decide where to spend your pay-per-click ad dollars.

The reviews are meant to be a starting point. We will cover the major characteristics and backgrounds of different search engines, some pros and cons associated with each one, the costs involved, and how highly rated specific search engines are via their Alexa ranking (a service that tracks websites and ranks them according to reach, traffic, and other factors).

Keep in mind your own particular goals, as discussed in the preceding chapters, as you look through the various pay-per-click search engine options available to you. If you know which features are most important to your marketing goals, be it a standard, simple PPC campaign, or an ad program for products that only a niche audience would be interested in, it will be easier to cut down the list of search engines that might fit your needs.

Using the information we provide in these short reviews should help you to narrow your choices. The next step for you is to visit the search engines themselves and fully investigate all the parameters.

In addition to reviews of a number of pay-per-click search engines, we'll also investigate comparison shopping sites and other markets just beginning to mature for other types of paid programs (such as pay-per-call advertising).

The Top Ten Pay-Per-Click Search Engines

The following 10 search engines are generally considered to be the best choices for pay-per-click advertising in terms of effectiveness. The price of an ad campaign on any of these search engines can vary greatly, depending on your individual requirements.

Each search engine will be briefly reviewed, with some detail provided on the operation of the search engine and its partnerships, the costs involved, and the pros and cons of using each search engine. Special product offerings will also be included, and information concerning minimum bids and deposit amounts will be listed.

1. **Google** (www.ppcbook.info/google)

 Since 1998, Google has grown from a two-man operation to what is arguably the largest and currently most popular search engine on the Internet. Most agree that Google garners more than 50% of all search traffic, with some estimates as high as 80%. The clean interface (recently patented), its broad access to products still in development (but relatively bug-free), and well-supported advertising package (AdWords) appeal to the majority of users and advertisers.

Starting an AdWords campaign is fairly straightforward, but a Starter Edition offers an even simpler interface (minus some features). Local search with advanced mapping via Google Earth, day-parting, geo-targeting, site targeting, free Google Analytics, the choice of contextual advertising, site map generation, Webmaster Central—the list of options and useful tools for advertisers to choose from is long and varied.

The Google paid ad display is the industry standard. An ad appears along the right side of the search results page or within content pages if content search is on. Recent changes in ranking parameters concentrate not just on bids, but also on the quality and relevance of your ad and the landing page associated with your ad (and indeed your entire website). This "Quality Score" concept has led to keywords becoming inactive for search plus reports of many huge jumps in keyword pricing.

The Google network includes entities such as AOL, Ask.com, Netscape, EarthLink, AT&T WorldNet, and CompuServe. Content partners include About.com, The New York Times, US News & World Report, and CBS Sportsline.

Pros: - Comprehensive, free web analytics package.

- Searchable support database and extensive collection of FAQs answer almost any question imaginable.

Cons: - Many factors relating to how "Quality Score" is defined can lead to disabling of keywords or high keyword costs.

- No clear definition of "invalid" clicks (fraudulent clicks).

Minimum Deposit – $5 USD

Minimum Bid Price – 1 cent

Minimum Monthly Spend Amount – none

Alexa Ranking – 3 (as of 02/2007)

2.   **Yahoo! Search Marketing** (www.ppcbook.info/yahoo)

 Yahoo! Search Marketing evolved from GoTo.com and Overture.

Yahoo! is in the middle of modifying its PPC offering via the Panama update. The previous strictly bid-for-position model will be supplanted by a system ranking ads based on how much an advertiser wants to spend. Advertisers enter a bid and a daily ad spend they are willing to pay, and Yahoo! will tell you what position in the sponsored listings is available for that amount of money. Estimates of the number of impressions, the number of clicks likely to occur and the total cost over 30 days are provided to help you plan.

Advertisers can specify goals they wish to reach with a campaign and Yahoo! Sponsored Search will provide information on how best to accomplish that given the keywords and creative available. Geotargeting can be applied to campaigns, instead of merely including the location in the ad creative for a search match. Campaigns can be scheduled by date.

Yahoo! can automatically select the versions of your ad that are most profitable and rotate those more often. Contextual advertising will, in the future, be based upon your ad and landing page content rather than keywords, which should provide more relevant listings. Ad listings will no longer take days to appear; most will be active within a few hours.

The partnership network includes AltaVista, InfoSpace, CNN, and others. With Content Match, it expands to include major content sites such as iVillage, The Weather Channel, and National Geographic.

Pros: -   ROI calculator tool available both for CPC and CPM ad setups.

-   Insert keyword feature dynamically inserts the keyword the bid is based upon into the ad's title or description.

Cons: -   Gradual transfer of accounts to new Panama setup could mean uncertain results for campaigns through first half of 2007.

Minimum Deposit – $5 USD

Minimum Bid Price – 10 cents

Minimum Monthly Spend Amount – none

Alexa Ranking – 1 (as of 02/2007)

3. Microsoft adCenter (www.ppcbook.info/microsoft)

Microsoft® adCenter

Microsoft adCenter is the online sales center for advertising options on Microsoft properties.

The PPC option is referred to as "P4P" or pay-for-performance ads. The US Live Search audience is identified as: "[on average] 45 years old, skews female, married, and 45 percent have children. They also earn high incomes (Avg. HHI $76.1K), and are well-educated, professionals—with an additional 4 percent being full-time students."

Having debuted relatively recently (May 2006 for the US), adCenter is still experimenting and gradually introducing options for advertisers. For example, contextual advertising is still an invitation-only option.

Sponsored ads are set up in a fairly basic bid-for-position format. It is possible to target your ad according to geographic location (not yet available for zip codes), day of the week, time of day or age/gender, but at additional cost above the basic keyword cost. Microsoft has an advantage over other search engines in its possession of a huge amount of personal and behavioral data through its various business units.

Dynamic text can be used with keywords to direct visitors to different landing pages.

Valuable tools are available or pending. Some of the more useful include: Keyword Forecast (which estimates impression count and demographics of one or more search terms), Forecasting Search Volume Seasonality, Search Funnels (help visualize search patterns), and Keyword Group Detection (finds similar keyword possibilities).

Pros: - Access to demographic info on millions of users who registered for MSN.net Passport or at other Microsoft sites.

Cons: - Quicklaunch program available (help with crafting ads and campaigns) but only if minimum daily spend is $30 or more.

- Although has a monthly spend tool that will allocate your spend throughout the month, no way to set a daily spend limit.

Minimum Deposit – $5 USD

Minimum Bid Price – 5 cents

Minimum Monthly Spend Amount – none

Alexa Ranking – 7 (as of 02/2007)

4.   Ask.com (www.ppcbook.info/ask)

Formerly known as Ask Jeeves, Ask.com is a part of IAC Search & Media (IAC/InterActive Corp.), which is head-quartered in Oakland, California. Ask is growing in popularity as an alternative search engine to Google and Yahoo!

The keyword auction model pricing is based upon what is called the "eCPM ranking," which is defined as the cost per click multiplied by the clickthrough rate. Your ad will be ranked using its eCPM rank in relation to other listings bidding on the same keyword(s).

The minimum cost per click needed to guarantee placement at the top of the sponsored listings is known as the reserve price and is based upon "market intelligence" and Ask.com CPCs already in place.

A forecast of expected ad spending for a month is provided to advertisers. Budgets can be set for a campaign, for a daily spend or for a month's worth of advertising.

The Ask.com network includes Mamma.com, InfoSpace, Dogpile, Excite, and CNET, among others. The most recent addition is the Lycos network.

AskCity.com is a nice local search option. Searchers like the answer-oriented set up of search engine results pages.

Pros: -   According to a June 2005 comScore report, Ask.com has a user overlap of only 21% with Yahoo! and 22% with Google, providing a good unique searcher base.

-    Account terminology similar to other search engines eases new account set up for those looking to experiment beyond Google and/or Yahoo!

-    Keyword bidding tool shows you the top 5 competitors.

Cons: -   Auction model is based upon eCPM ranking (which is CPC x CTR).

Minimum Deposit – $15 USD

Minimum Bid Price – 5 cents

Minimum Monthly Spend Amount – none

Alexa Ranking – 209 (as of 02/2007)

5.   ABCSearch (www.ppcbook.info/abcsearch)

ABCSearch has struggled back from an unfortunate reputation as an adware source. It is a subsidiary of Internext Media Corp. and now one of the fastest-growing search engines (Encino, California).

ABCSearch uses the classic PPC model, where an advertiser identifies keywords and bids in real time for ranking based on the "per click" cost. The higher you bid on a keyword, the higher your ad will appear in search results pages. Bid gap problems are eliminated via a dynamic bid program, which will set your bid at 1 cent above the second ad position, up to the bid you have identified as your maximum. Maximum bids can be set for individual keywords or across your entire campaign (if the advertiser feels all keywords are of equal importance to the campaign).

Geotargeting is available for the US and Canada, as well as a number of other countries. Local search at the state, city or "area" level is supported.

Late in 2006, ABCSearch introduced the proprietary program ClickShield to help prevent click fraud. Using information gathered about network traffic patterns, each click is "scrubbed" against this user info and other methods of statistical analysis to identify fraudulent clicks. ABCSearch believes that 85% of click fraud is affiliate-related and will block traffic from individual affiliates if ClickShield identifies a problem.

Their network is comprised of more than 300 niche search engines, including Kanoodle, Brainfox, ISEDN, SearchWho, ExactWebsites, MetaWebSearch, and others. ABCSearch handles 2.5 billion searches per month. Contextual ads are offered via their Adentify product (beta).

Pros: -   Auto rebilling keeps your account replenished once it reaches a specified minimum.

-    $25 payment for referral of a PPC advertiser who sets up an account.

Cons: -   Approval of ads can take up to 24 hours.

Minimum Deposit – $25 USD

Minimum Bid Price – 5 cents

Minimum Monthly Spend Amount – none

Alexa Ranking – 1,950 (as of 02/2007)

6.   Search*feed* (www.ppcbook.info/searchfeed**)**

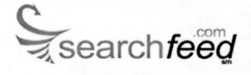

New Jersey-based Search*feed* first began operation late in the year 2000. Traffic quality is monitored by TrafficAnalyst, its traffic-ranking software. Search*feed* relies on a technique of personally and thoroughly researching any potential web advertiser and providing assistance and software tools to help each advertiser target the most relevant traffic for their site.

With a starting bid of 1 cent for many keywords, Search*feed* has built a reputation as a solid base from which to run an effective marketing campaign, especially for smaller businesses.

Geo-targeting is available, as are with tools that statistics on keyword search frequency over the network, ROI estimates, and campaign cost estimates. A bid research tool allows you to check the current cost of keywords you would like to add to your campaign. Real-time statistics on click activity are standard and bid gap management is available upon request.

Although relevance is considered very important in the editorial review of ads, there is obviously more flexibility than some other search engines (it is stated that a campaign will be rejected if "over 50%" of its keywords are judged "irrelevant"). Search*feed*'s network is comprised of a wide variety of partners.

Pros: -   In addition to the usual tools and reports, a number of useful tools help gauge the past performance of keywords, ROI, and the total campaign cost.

        -    Users like the intuitive interface and low-cost keywords, as well as responsive customer service.

Cons: -   Account activation takes at least two days, sometimes longer, due to stringent checks of financial information from advertisers.

        -    Minimum deposit is non-refundable if you cancel your account at some point in the future.

Minimum Deposit – $25 USD

Minimum Bid Price – 1 cent

Minimum Monthly Spend Amount – none

Alexa Ranking – 4,477 (as of 02/2007)

7.   MIVA - FindWhat (www.ppcbook.info/miva)

FindWhat became MIVA in 2004. It has three divisions—Media (offering performance advertising options such as PPC), Small Business (website solutions), and Direct (private branded software solutions). Its main strengths lie in its adaptability, its various arrangements with other search properties, and a European presence through Espotting.

MIVA offers two options for advertisers—pay per click and pay per call. MIVA was the first to add pay per call to advertising options in 2004. Powering over 2 billion queries a month, MIVA runs PPC networks in the US, UK, France, Germany, Spain and Italy. MIVA operates a bid-for-position auction where advertisers see the actual bid price. In Europe, MIVA displays advertisers' brand logos as part of their PPC ads. PPC accounts are easy and intuitive to create and follow the classic setup. A suite of tools includes bid optimizing and auto-bidding, ROI analysis, and automatic re-funding of your account once the balance drops below a set amount. They also have a good reputation for click fraud detection.

MIVA's PPC ads will appear on sites such as Search.com, InfoSpace, Eurekster, CNET.com and Searchfeed. MIVA has also maintained the FindWhat web search site. MIVA MC (Monetization Center) offers an affiliate program that can place ads next to your content, within your content (via inline ads), or on your own search results pages.

Pros: -   Well-established pay-per-call option (the details of page setup and time of day your ads appear are customizable). In 2006, MIVA launched Pay-Per-Text Ads for SMS text messaging through Britain's directory assistance, 118 118.

-    Advertisers can choose timeframe from which they wish to receive summaries of their account—daily, weekly, monthly.

Cons: -   Keyword generator only available for UK Ad Center and doesn't specify source of data generated.

-    Bid change frequency limit of 60 minutes.

Minimum Deposit – $25 USD

Minimum Bid Price – 5 cents

Minimum Monthly Spend Amount – none

Alexa Ranking – 39,928 (as of 02/2007)

8.　　**7Search** (http://www.ppcbook.info/7search)

7Search promotes itself as the search engine for advertisers who have "low profit margin" business categories and can't afford to pay more than 10 cents per click. In business since 1999, 7Search claims a better ROI than either Google or Yahoo! and over 1.5 million searches per hour.

The setup is fairly standard and options, reporting, and account management tools provided are in line with other niche search engines. Unfortunately, 7Search doesn't offer geo-targeting, so some non-US traffic will inevitably occur, especially since the costs for PPC ads are quite low.

Click fraud technology is an integral part of the package. A handy keyword suggestion tool brings up related keywords, the number of searches, and the cost for placement at the top 5 ad positions. The keyword activity lookup tool will show the same information, but this time for the keyword you are intending to use. Both keyword tools use data from the previous month.

AccessoryAd program places ads on sites with related content, but not competitive with your keywords. Keyword bids start at 1 cent and network-level bidding is available so an advertiser can bid for placement at the top of 7Search's network partner sites. An ad will appear within minutes of sign-up and 7Search's network encompasses up to 35% of the top search engines.

Pros:　-　35% of the top 150 search engines use 7Search results. 7Search is reported to pay out over $750,000 each month to partners and affiliates.

-　One of the few PPC search engines to accept PayPal.

-　Emails you when your account drops to an estimated three days worth of click money.

Cons:　-　Only available for English websites in English-speaking countries, apparently to help detect and deter click fraud.

Minimum Deposit – $25 USD

Minimum Bid Price – 1 cent

Minimum Monthly Spend Amount – none

<u>Alexa Ranking</u> – 4,563 (as of 02/2007)

9. Enhance Interactive (www.ppcbook.info/enhance)

Originally founded as ah-ha.com in 1999, Enhance Interactive was owned by eFamily of Utah and originally concentrated on being a family friendly search engine. It became a wholly owned subsidiary of Marchex, Inc. in 2003 (also the owner of GoClick). Enhance's traffic distribution consists of Marchex's Vertical Network of over 200,000 websites, as well as search partners such as Dogpile, Metacrawler, and Snap.com.

Enhance offers two options for PPC customers—a package where you construct your own campaign or an option where an account manager performs campaign optimization for you. If you choose to have your PPC campaign created by Enhance, you will be assigned an individual to work with you personally on account optimization for the relatively low fee of $99.

Clicks start at 3 cents and, for many keywords, wind up lower than at leading search engines. The account management interface is intuitive and easy to use, with detailed reporting options. Enhance has recently stepped up efforts to monitor its highly automated ad listing process in order to catch click fraud and other suspect activity as quickly as possible. They also offer a paid inclusion program and contextual advertising options.

Pros: - Customer service is a priority and includes Live Chat support.

- LogoLinks program at $9.95 per month. The small logo next to your ad is an added degree of personalization.

- AccuMatch system expands keywords to include plurals, misspellings, and (most importantly) simple phrases.

Cons: - Results are listed with highest PPC bidders first, followed by other PPC ads and then organic results—a confusing presentation.

Minimum Deposit – $50 USD

Minimum Bid Price – 3 cents

Minimum Monthly Spend Amount – none

Alexa Ranking – 4,836 (as of 02/2007)

10.   Findology (www.ppcbook.info/findology)

Findology.com, a part of TrafficAds Media, Inc., has a clean, Google-type look to it. With more than 2 billion searches per month, Findology's key advantage is its partnerships with a number of channels typically not attached to other search engines.

Their PPC search advertising is the typical auction bid for click, but they also offer a "guaranteed" ROI program, where you only pay Findology upon conversions (although here you will pay a portion of each conversion instead of a per-click charge), with billing occurring once your account reaches $100.

Traffic sources are identified in reports, allowing you to evaluate sources and request that your ads not be sent in the future to sources that are not converting well for your campaigns. FraudID technology fights click fraud.

Five different types of search are available: Web, News, People, Shopping and Research. Running the Web search for "computer monitors," we received results showing sponsored ads above the organic search results (which had a fair number of duplicate entries for the same web page) and along the right side of the page. The Shopping search defaults back to the Web search. The last tab on the Findology search box is "More," which takes you to the Findology Portal—an impressive array of news, weather, movies, travel info and search.

User comments are generally as one would expect—lower amount of traffic than Google or Yahoo!, but often better ROI and more conversions.

Pros: -   Portal is attractive and integrates the search bar with useful information.

-   Referral fee of $25 for referring new advertisers.

Cons: -   Duplicate listings in search results.

Minimum Deposit – $25 USD

Minimum Bid Price – 3 cents

Minimum Monthly Spend Amount – none

Alexa Ranking – 8,876 (as of 02/2007)

Second-Tier Pay-Per-Click Search Engines

Outside of the Top Ten, there are a large number of PPC search engines that are generally classified as "second tier." The term is usually defined as small search engine sites that typically have a relatively small amount of traffic.

However, despite the smaller amounts of traffic to second-tier PPC search engines, they may be just what you are looking for. The cost to mount an ad campaign is generally quite low, and some second-tier search engines have partnerships with websites that may be directly connected to the market you are interested in.

Sometimes the best place for a novice to start in pay-per-click advertising is with a second-tier search engine, where you can hone your skills at keyword bidding, etc., in an atmosphere that requires less personal attention because the traffic is lower. If you investigate and find a second-tier search engine that looks as if it will fit your needs, and you decide to invest a small amount of money in a trial run, be prepared for the small amount of traffic you may receive and the fewer sales you will make.

Second-tier search engines provide a good opportunity for you to spread your ad dollars across a few different search engines, while you might be limited by your budget to only one of the Top 10 if you took that route. Therefore, they can be a great place to learn more about the process at a relatively low cost.

Keep in mind that "second tier" does not mean "second rate." Some of the 200-plus search engines that currently fit into this category can perform quite well for you and the lower cost will increase your ROI when you do convert a visitor into a buyer.

> Second-tier search engines do not mean "second rate." Many of them actually perform quite well and are cheaper than the Top 10.

Many second-tier engines have almost all the tools and features of the Top 10 and, over time, will unseat one of the Top 10 if enough enhancements are made. Quality of service and delivery of results may improve their situation online, so word of mouth may bring them increased traffic. One key aspect in pay-per-click advertising is that it is always changing, so be prepared for some of the search engines reviewed in the next few pages to climb into the Top 10 as the year 2007 continues.

We are providing reviews of 10 second-tier PPC search engines to give you an idea of the kind of diversity available to you if you wish to experiment with a smaller property, especially if you are just beginning to investigate online advertising.

1.   AdOn Networks (myGeek) (www.ppcbook.info/adon)

AdOn Networks (formerly myGeek) offers up more than 155 million unique users and 5.5 billion searches each month. Three types of ads are available: popunder ads (keyword targeting in a CPM environment), text-based display ads (bids are based on cost per view), and PPC search listings. PPC listings start at 5 cents per click. "Advertiser Retargeting" option delivers your ad to previous visitors when they visit websites in the AdOn Network in the future.

Search listings utilize a bid-for-traffic method, where advertisers pay for the maximum amount of traffic they wish, setting limits within their budgets that can go as low as 5 cents per click. Traffic Estimator Tool helps estimate traffic using historical search data.

Two click fraud fighting features are an option to deactivate traffic sources that aren't converting to par and "competitor block" (covering up to eight websites). Good, in-depth reporting and assistance readily available from Advertiser Services reps for optimizing ad campaigns.

Alexa Ranking – 9,245 (as of 02/2007)

2.   ChaCha (www.ppcbook.info/chacha)

ChaCha.com, launched in September 2006, is different from the typical search engine, since it uses live human beings as search guides, free of charge, to users having difficulty finding what they want via organic search. The interface is very reminiscent of Google, and the site itself is clean and uncluttered. Navigation of the site is not as intuitive as it could be, but future versions will no doubt address those issues.

Organic search results for ChaCha are pulled from unspecified partner sites, and the quality of these results is similar to a typical metacrawler site. Sponsored results appear to be mainly (if not exclusively) from Google AdWords at this point. ChaCha does offer advertising opportunities for cost per click and cost per action, as well as more traditional banner and all varieties of video ads.

What makes advertising on ChaCha different is that ads are shown adjacent to the chat window while the user waits for the search guide to put together the search results behind the scenes. With little else to do but wait, ChaCha's sales pitch is that users will be more likely to look at the ads that come up during the waiting period and, hopefully, click on them and potentially purchase something from the advertiser.

Alexa Ranking – 8,743 (as of 02/2007)

3. Clicksor (www.ppcbook.info/clicksor)

Clicksor is a Toronto, Canada-based division of YesUp Ecommerce Solutions, Inc., originally founded in 1999. Clicksor differs in concentrating solely on contextual ads via their "Content Targeting" technology, with different ad display options under different cost metrics.

Clicksor offers screening for "suspicious" traffic and a real-time management system. A private label option was just launched in December 2006, and targeting by country is available.

Clicksor is partnered with a number of minority web destinations and some niche-oriented locations that may offer decent traffic if your business fits into those channels. Links to Hispanic and Asian networks could be useful as these sectors grow in online importance. Also partnered with Tickle, YouTube, CommunityConnect, MiniClip, UserPlane, and MetaCafe.

Alexa Ranking – 1,795 (as of 02/2007)

4. GoClick (www.ppcbook.info/goclick)

GoClick is part of the Marchex group, which also owns Enhance Interactive and TrafficLeader (a search marketing agency). Go-Click has a standard vertical, category-style listing format with topics to narrow search results. The network receives approximately 6 billion searches each month, and they work with more than 50 partner networks.

A plus is their emphasis on "unique" clicks, where they promise to only charge one time for a click from a specific visitor in a 24-hour period, no matter how many times that visitor may click on your ad.

GoClick's main selling point is their low, 1-cent per click starting bids with no minimum ad spend.

New accounts can be opened with as little as $10, and a daily spend limit can be specified.

Nice beginner's guide on the site and access to Top 100 Terms tool for keyword research. Bid gap management is not provided at this time, but click costs are shown on results pages (all listings are sponsored).

Easy to open up an account with, but as with all smaller PPC properties, advertisers need to have realistic expectations.

Alexa Ranking – 11,608 (as of 02/2007)

5. GenieKnows (www.ppcbook.info/genieknows)

GenieKnows now has a Google-like search interface, with searches available in five specific verticals—Health, Games, Business, Local (still in beta, but offering general, specific and distance-based options), and People (provided by Reunion.com). Depending upon which tab the searcher has enabled, different results for the same search term will appear.

Lots of recent changes include the addition of day-parting and budgeting features and a keyword selection tool that returns keywords based on past searches on the GenieKnows.com network itself. A new "Network Boost" option lets you change your bid to match the high bid across the entire network ("Since the majority of our traffic comes from outside of our site, this small change can make a large difference in the amount of traffic you receive."). Gambling ads are permitted.

Serves up more than 1 billion searches per month across their network. Users like their detailed reports (stats are available in real-time) and the clean interface. Minimum bids start at 1 cent, with no minimum spend, but a somewhat large $50 minimum to open an account.

Alexa Ranking – 53,570 (as of 02/2007)

6. Kanoodle (www.ppcbook.info/kanoodle)

In late 2006, Kanoodle rebranded as Seevast, keeping its search advertising component, while the contextual, behavioral and local advertising offerings are now handled by Pulse360 (in a wide variety of sponsored ad options).

The Kanoodle website is filled with lots of clear content and functions that allow you to closely monitor your PPC campaign. KeywordTarget is Kanoodle's sponsored links product geared towards searchers. Ads appear on a wide network of search engines (CNET's Search.com and InfoSpace properties, including Mamma, WebCrawler and Dogpile).

There's a keyword suggestion tool for those who want more help in beginning their campaigns. Kanoodle also offers assistance with creating custom listings, including titles and descriptions.

A simple step-by-step interface makes adding new listings a snap, and once approved, it is easy to tweak ad copy, change bids and make other changes. Listings can be scheduled to go on and off at predetermined times, bids can be set to keep pace with competitors, and spending caps help keep budgets under control.

Alexa Ranking – 14,136 (as of 02/2007)

7.   LookSmart (www.ppcbook.info/looksmart)

LookSmart is a directory-style site organized by category based in San Francisco and founded in 1996. The search page features a list of local articles and web resources that are automatically generated from the user's IP address, and an area to "find, save, and share what you like." Ads are distributed on their 180+ vertical search sites and network of partners (includes InfoSpace, CNET, Snap.com, Mamma, and more). Click fraud is targeted via the TrueLead™ traffic purification process. Their Health channel has 3.3 million unique visitors per month.

Great collection of how-to material on their website and very informative newsletter and webinars are available. LookSmart AdCenter offers lots of reporting and campaign management options. Staff is also available for optimization assistance. Accounts are very easy to set up and maintain. The Targeting Optimizer allows you to look for little-used keywords that may be bargain-priced in the marketplace.

Account refill amount must be at least three times your daily budget. Pricing of keyword listings is calculated using the maximum CPC and CTR, so account balances should be watched carefully.

Alexa Ranking – 2,721 (as of 02/2007)

8.   Mamma (www.ppcbook.info/mamma)

Placement in Mamma's search network is a little more complicated than most. The top three advertisers bidding on a specific keyword will be included in Mamma.com, and others ranked fourth or below will have their ads placed on the Mamma Media Solutions network. If two or more advertisers bid on the same keyword at the same price, the ads are ranked based on a first-come, first-served basis.

There is a handy keyword estimator tool available at the site which will show you the estimated monthly searches for keywords. Optimization of accounts is free of charge and the online client center is available 24/7. Click fraud is handled with a variety of checks and balances, including allowing only one click per IP address in 24 hours to be charged to your account. Relevancy is important to Mamma—its "Rsort" program checks for duplicate results and displays the one with the most duplicates, reducing search engine spam. Geo-targeting is available.

Current minimum bids start at 5 cents. The Mamma website has a variety of targeted search parameters (image, health, jobs, yellow pages, white pages), as well as a toolbar and a desktop search feature for users.

Alexa Ranking – 3,002 (as of 02/2007)

9.   Search123 (www.ppcbook.info/search123)

Launched in 2000, Search123 is part of ValueClick, which also offers search engine marketing services. Their traffic is described as "made up of hundreds of high-quality content sites, directories and search engines that generate hundreds of millions of searches and millions of qualified clicks to our advertisers each month." Much of their organic traffic originates in the Simpli.com network and they have a good presence in Hispanic content networks.

Account set up is uncomplicated and free assistance is available either for set up or optimization of ads. Existing account changes take place in real-time, and Search123 offers click quality monitoring, spending limits, bid management, and automatic funding of accounts.

Terms of services emphasize need for relevant content on advertiser websites. Adult content sites are permitted (within limits). Minimum amount to open an account is $50 USD, but there is no minimum spend requirement.

Alexa Ranking – 68,698 (as of 02/2007)

10.   Snap.com (www.ppcbook.info/snap)

Snap is an innovative search engine that offers users a preview of the website associated with an ad listing to help searchers pick and choose sites to click on most appropriate to their needs, reducing the number of clicks on your ad by searchers with no interest in your offerings. Chosen as one of TIME magazine's "50 Coolest Websites of 2006," Snap is a service of Perfect Market Technologies, Inc., a part of Idealab (originator of Overture, which was acquired by Yahoo! in 2003).

In addition to a standard PPC model, Snap offers a cost-per-action option, where advertisers only pay if a user completes a specified action, such as a purchase, signing up for a newsletter, or asking for more information. The sponsored listings appear mixed in with organic listings, using an algorithm that takes into account conversion ratings, post-click behavior, text and link analysis, etc.

There is a $50 non-refundable sign-up deposit required for a Snap account. The site is very attractive, and the website preview option (as well as the ability for searchers to vote on whether or not a site is useful), puts a slightly different slant on the search experience. Image search capabilities have recently been added and the Snap Preview Anywhere tool is available for placement on WordPress blogs and other websites.

Alexa Ranking – 3,792 (as of 02/2007)

Pay-Per-Inclusion Search Engines

Pay per inclusion used to be the prime method of "buying" your way onto a search engine on the Internet, starting in the late 1990s. At that point, with less competition on search engines because fewer companies had a web presence, natural rankings often worked, but paid inclusion was a guaranteed way to get listed on a search engine. It usually was a one-time fee per year for guaranteed inclusion in the search engine's index of sites.

Because pay-per-inclusion ads are virtually indistinguishable to the average user, as the Internet grew as a commercial enterprise, the market gradually began to move away from paid inclusion, for a number of reasons. For example, the development of search engines whose ranking was based on algorithms and robot crawls, and who did not offer paid inclusion as an option, led to a perception by many that these "organic" results were more "genuine" than listings that appeared in search results as a result of payment.

However, there are benefits to using paid inclusion, the major one being that it bypasses the typical delay of weeks in getting your website listed on a search engine. If you enter a pay-per-inclusion program on a search engine, your site is usually included within a few days and the search engine robot will regularly crawl your site as well, so changes you make to your site will be reflected in a timely manner.

Consequently, for many advertisers, paid inclusion has been a method to get online quickly instead of relying on SEO and robot crawls to do their magic before having their websites show up under relevant searches.

Paid inclusion underwent a total reversal in general opinion soon after Google began to flourish. Google has consistently said they would never offer paid inclusion because they believe it taints the search process by artificially ranking paid inclusion sites higher. Search engines offering paid inclusion took the opposite view, but in general, the Google viewpoint prevailed and search engines moved away from paid inclusion.

In March of 2004, Yahoo! reopened the debate by announcing their decision to include paid listings again in their search results, stating that there would be no ranking advantage from a pay-per-inclusion submission. The end result of the strong debate over this strategy was that Yahoo! retained paid listings, and Google reasserted its position (in its IPO, late in 2004) that it believes natural search is the only guarantee of a "free and open" marketplace.

Although Yahoo! is still the only standard search engine that technically offers pay per inclusion, since it is partnered with so many other search engines, paid listings are often found in many search engine results.

In fact, paid inclusion can be a cheap supplement to keep among your online marketing strategies, especially if the cost per click of your keywords is making it difficult to maintain your pay-per-click position. People still do act on general search results, so some analysts do suggest advertisers consider experimenting with the Yahoo! program, especially if you are finding PPC on your keywords out of your dollar reach.

Remember, however, that with paid inclusion, clickthrough rates may be higher. As well, the rising popularity of PPC ads leads analysts to believe that at least 40% of all conversions come from pay-per-click ads, a trend that is expected to increase.

> Pay per inclusion can prove to be a good supplement to a well-rounded search engine advertising campaign.

Like any paid form of advertising online, and despite the feeling many have that paid listings are tainted, it can't hurt to get your website listed with those search engines that support pay per inclusion, as long as the cost is in line with your budget.

International PPC Search Engines

Although many advertisers in the United States think there is little value in investing ad dollars in PPC search engines in the international market, research shows that this is quickly changing. Interest in placing PPC ads on international search engines is increasing with the increasing presence of Google and Yahoo! search engines in a large number of countries throughout the world.

Although you may think that you cannot compete in an international marketplace, there is definitely a market for US products from consumers abroad. It may not be a large source of sales, but keyword costs can be lower in such markets, thus your overall conversion rate may be worth the investment.

The acquisition of Espotting, a UK-based search engine, by FindWhat (which has now become MIVA) in 2004, and its subsequent merging of international listing options into their

> If you plan to market your business in another country, make sure to create a mirror of your site in the appropriate language.

PPC program, offers a simple and familiar way to experiment in the international market. Mirago.com also offers a robust international presence. Many other smaller search engines have international listings interspersed in their results.

Some advertisers just do not want to become involved in the additional factors involved in international sales, but if your company already has an international presence, pay-per-click advertising for international websites is a natural fit.

Most search engines offering international placement to US-based websites only do so for countries that are English-speaking. There is a valid reason for this— if your PPC ad in Korean entices someone to click on your ad and they are taken to an English-only website, it is doubtful that the ad will be appreciated by the visitor. This can rebound, not just on the advertiser, but also on the search engine's reputation.

Therefore, if you plan on exploring the PPC market in non-English-speaking search engines, be sure that your website has an excellent mirror site in the language(s) of the country you are targeting.

The Spanish/Hispanic market has been moving forward and is positioned for huge growth. Therefore, experimenting on Spanish-based PPC search engines with a professionally translated mirror website may be quite effective. The Hispanic population in the US has become such a significant and growing part of the market that expansion into Spanish versions of your website and involvement in Latin American search engines is an option to consider for almost any advertiser.

Niche Pay-Per-Click Search Engines

Niche search engines are defined as those that cater to a specific market or industry instead of the general marketplace. Some of the smaller PPC search engines are in fact niche engines, because they have found that by concentrating on getting advertisers who are all selling related products and services on one search engine, traffic specific to that market area will be highly targeted. Thus, visitors to niche search engines often are more motivated and more likely to convert into buyers than visitors to general PPC search engines.

Of course, with a niche search engine, pay-per-click advertising may not be as worthwhile, particularly if the engine is small and is not capable of delivering enough traffic to justify the expense and time needed for an ad campaign.

The trick for the advertiser wishing to investigate PPC on niche search engines is to find a niche search engine that has quality, targeted, natural listings, because their visitors will consider a paid ad valid if they value the utility of the search engine itself. On the other hand, if a niche search engine's organic results bring up too many listings unrelated to the original search term, perhaps due to a lack of advertisers and few partnerships with content-rich search engines, it is questionable that your ROI from an ad campaign will be sufficient.

A fast-growing segment in niche search engines concerns health topics. For example, the topic of fitness is one that most people are concerned about to some extent, and fitness-related search engines have sprung up and begun to attract advertisers via pay-per-click options. One such search engine, www.fitness.com (powered by Ah-ha.com) offers pay-per-click listings within its directory-style search engine starting at 5 cents per click with a $50 deposit.

Even though it is a niche search engine, this fitness-related site offers real-time statistics and the ability to change your keywords at any time, with only a couple of days to get your ad online.

Niche search engines should be a part of your marketing campaign if your product/service fits into a certain category. Many places on the Internet

> Look for niche-specific PPC search engines in your industry.

have listings of niche search engines specific to particular industries, and you may find that your ROI from such a source is equal to, and sometimes better than, competing in the general market.

People who are very interested in a specific industry, be it a type of product or an interest or hobby (such as fitness, weddings, collectibles, travel, or genealogy research), will look for niche search engines or hear of them from fellow enthusiasts. If the search engine is well organized, attractive, and returns relevant results, those visitors will come back again and again.

If you decide to investigate niche search engines, do ensure that the results are relevant and content-rich by doing some investigation on your own before committing to any PPC campaign. Without quality results, a niche engine has little chance of being a good place to put your advertising dollars, because traffic will be too low to provide enough conversions to justify your time investment.

Niche search engines can be just one more tool in your arsenal of putting together a PPC campaign. You can concentrate on a larger search engine if you find your ROI is good with them, and experiment with niche search engines to see if they are worth investing more ad dollars in.

Comparison Shopping PPC Search Engines

Although comparison shopping search engines have been a fixture on the Internet for a number of years now, it's only in the last couple of years that they have become an increasingly popular area for experimentation by advertisers.

Most comparison shopping search engines provide a lot of information to shoppers to help make informed decisions, including not just merchant reviews, but also reviews from magazines and "experts" (most often websites that sell the products). Results pages can usually be sorted by the different headings, such as price.

Once you click on a seller or product, you are usually taken to the seller's website to purchase the item there. Comparison shopping search engines do not conduct actual transactions; instead they act primarily as an information center as well as a pay-per-click search engine, sending the visitor to the advertiser's website to make the actual purchase.

Merchant information is available via a simple click underneath each individual product for sale, and often reviews of merchant/advertisers are available compiled from user feedback. In fact, most comparison shopping search engines rely at least somewhat on users to report any differences in pricing, product availability, or other details when they actually check the product out on the seller's website.

Some larger sellers arrange data feeds to the search engine, but smaller advertisers need to ensure that their product-line data is kept up to date to avoid negative user reports and perhaps removal from the site.

Shopping comparison sites are becoming more popular with consumers because of the variety of information they offer in one place, thus saving the consumer valuable time.

If you wish to advertise on a shopping comparison search engine, you will probably have two options. The first is basically pay-per-click advertising for your product(s), for which you pay a standard set amount per click to be included in a specific category.

The process of advertising is usually very easy, often with a step-by-step walkthrough that leads you through creating your listing, setting the pricing, methods of payment you will accept, adding an image, describing the product, and so on.

Although setup is usually free, there are various charges associated with most options that are needed for a competitive listing, and restrictions on terms such as what kind of payment options you can offer.

Sometimes your ads are limited to certain categories, and the search engine charges you when an item is sold. An example of pricing might be $1 plus 4.75% of the sales price, including shipping and handling charges. In all cases, you are responsible for ensuring that the proper taxes are charged, collected, and delivered to the appropriate authorities.

Many offer sophisticated reporting to their advertisers, and now provide data not only on the number of sales, but also to cost-per-click analysis and ROI conversion tracking.

Sales are usually monitored, as are purchases and users, in order to assign you to a category that dictates your maximum selling limit for the next 30-day period. You may not list anything for sale at a price above this limit, which helps ensure that only active sellers are participating. Comparison shopping sites are concerned with maintaining a high-quality shopping experience for their visitors—thus, many restrictions and rules are tracked and enforced.

The second option for selling, especially if you wish to sell in higher volumes, is to become a merchant. At this level, more tools and options are available to you, but you still need to adhere to numerous rules and constraints.

Usually, you will need to work with an account manager and pay a setup fee to integrate the data feed necessary to keep your sales information as up-to-date as possible. The usual tracking tools are provided in the program—number of sales, tracking of sales in a close to real-time environment, etc.—with reports available by category, brand, or product.

Comparison shopping sites act as an intermediary in all ways, sending you to the seller/advertiser to make the actual purchase. They typically have a multitude of rules and restrictions, and additional costs and penalties, so sellers need to keep track of a lot of information in order to manage their accounts and not lose sight of their ROI.

Typically, pricing for advertising is on a pay-per-click basis, but with a specific cost per category, rather than keyword bidding. Since visitors to such a site are motivated to buy, many factors may already have been decided by them (such as brand name, price they are looking for, unique features, etc.). Because they have the ability to sort a results page by factors such as price or availability of the product, ranking on the page at some point moves beyond the control of the advertiser or the search engine itself.

Market expectations are that comparison shopping search engines will continue to grow and evolve in the near future, mostly in response to the success of pay per click on standard search engines.

> Because shopping search engines offer such a wealth of information to the consumer, they can cut down the buying cycle from 12 weeks to one day.

Shopping sites offer so much information in one place for the consumer that listings on them can cut the usual buying cycle timeframe of 12 weeks down to one day. Impulse purchases are also often made as visitors browse through pages of results with images of the products and all the relevant information they need to make a buying decision right at their fingertips.

Smaller advertisers may feel that the brand name sellers dominate comparison shopping PPC search engines, and to some extent that is so. However, if your pricing is competitive, your listings are up-to-date, and your website has an easy and intuitive shopping cart, many smaller advertisers report good conversions on shopping sites.

Although there are literally hundreds of these types of sites on the Internet, a few do stand out from the rest—namely PriceGrabber.com, NexTag.com, Shopzilla.com (formerly BizRate), and mySimon.com (a CNET property).

These types of search engines should be investigated if you sell products and want to compete with the "big guys." You may be pleasantly surprised at the results in this type of shopping environment. As always, keep in mind that with pay-per-click advertising, diversity in the types of search engines you place your advertising dollars on is often the key to success.

Pay-Per-Call Online Advertising

A new version of paid advertising emerged in 2004, with the introduction of the pay-per-call model. This type of ad is very similar to a classic PPC ad, except that your listing includes a toll-free number to call to reach you.

Some search engines bring up a page specific to your business (usually included at no extra charge to the advertiser) if the visitor clicks on the ad. You are not charged for the clickthrough unless the visitor actually makes the call. The toll-free number then redirects the visitor to your actual phone number, and you receive the phone call from the interested buyer at your business location.

The parameters of bidding on keywords or categories (which are usually high, in the $2-$20 range) are augmented by specification of which degree of geographic coverage you wish—national, regional or local.

Pay-per-call advertising is of particular interest for those businesses that do not have a website or do not want to invest in setting up and maintaining a website, but yet want to take advantage of advertising on the Internet.

Other companies find it a useful addition to their PPC campaigns, particularly to avoid charges on their pay-per-click campaigns by those users merely seeking a phone number to reach the advertiser.

A clear advantage is that once an advertiser has a prospect on the phone, they are in their "comfort zone" as far as sales are concerned, particularly smaller businesses. They are used to selling over the phone and the direct contact means that they can answer a prospect's questions in real-time.

> Pay-per-call advertising is a great opportunity for businesses that prefer to deal with their prospects and clients the old-fashioned way—over the phone.

Although pay per call is still in its relative infancy, recent events point to its potential for growth online. For one, Google is beginning to integrate a calling feature into Google Maps. Searchers click on a link next to the phone number for a business located on Google Maps and, once they enter their own phone number, are connected to the business at no charge.

Google pays for the calls (unless you are connecting via your mobile). Businesses should, at the very least, consider taking advantage of this no-cost offering in Google and complete the information necessary to get this linked up to a business listing via the Local Business Center at Google.

If you are interested in pursuing this type of advertising, MIVA (formerly FindWhat) is the leader amongst the larger search engines in offering pay-per-call options (although the trial program by Google bears some watching). Pay per call is also a hallmark of some of the Internet yellow pages sites and many local shopping directories.

Conclusion

This chapter introduced you to the leading pay-per-click search engines, as well as a variety of other click-based types of advertising currently available on the Internet. Given the growth potential of pay per click, an advertiser should carefully research their options before committing to any ad campaign, and small-to-medium-sized businesses (with smaller ad budgets than the large companies online) have to be especially careful.

It is also good to consider spreading your ad dollars into different types of PPC advertising. This can be as simple as placing PPC ads on different search engines and analyzing the results to see which program provides you with a higher ROI. You should also consider who provided the best customer service experience for you, the advertiser.

These are key components in any advertising campaign, but they are especially important in pay-per-click advertising, where the online factor takes marketing your product/service to a whole new level—a level where the difference between a successful and unsuccessful campaign may be affected by more factors than typical in offline advertising.

Smaller businesses, in particular, are often reluctant to enter the online paid advertising marketplace, feeling that they have little chance of success, given the competition. However, many small businesses are succeeding in garnering successful ROI by carefully investigating and exploring the different options available to them. As well, the integration of a local flavor to pay-per-click advertising should serve the small-to-medium-sized business community well.

Finding the right search engine(s) for your online marketing campaign is one of the most important tasks, but you must also investigate tools and methods for keeping track of the performance of those campaigns. In past chapters, we've talked in general about third-party tools and services being available to help you double-check or augment the information that your search engine provides to you on the performance of your ad(s).

Following a path similar to that taken here, the next chapter introduces you to some tools and services that are available to help pay-per-click advertisers with their ad campaigns.

Chapter 11 – Pay-Per-Click Tools

Placing an ad on pay-per-click search engines is only half the battle. The other half, as we've discussed in past chapters, is ensuring that your ad campaigns actually generate a profit for your business and are not just a waste of ad dollars.

How PPC Tools Can Make Managing an Ad Campaign Easier

A number of tools have been developed to help advertisers manage their ad campaigns. Some are included with your pay-per-click ad campaigns, but others are available from third parties. Both can be useful in running and optimizing PPC campaigns.

The management and tracking tools provided by your PPC search engine are often impressive. However, if you want to be certain that the information you receive is as accurate a reflection of reality as possible, you should consider investing in one or more third-party tools designed to validate the data from your search engine or to supply information that they do not provide.

Depending upon your individual skill set and experience, such tools can take a lot of the burden of manual checking of ad campaign data off of the individual advertiser. Although you should always keep an eye on your ad campaigns, and manual checking of your campaign should be routine, the use of an ROI tracking tool, for example, can save you a lot of time normally spent calculating the bottom line on any number of ad campaigns.

Thus, whether you are a novice and feel better having an expert backing up your observations of how your ad campaign is progressing, or a seasoned PPC campaigner who is managing dozens of comparative ad campaigns, independent third-party tools are useful and can make management of your ad campaign(s) easier and less time-consuming.

User forums are full of entries from advertisers who have seen profitable ad campaigns turn into nightmare, account-draining entities within a few days with no real explanation from their PPC search engine. A third-party tool may provide you with the answer behind such a dilemma, specifically because it is the only unbiased partner in the trio of the advertiser, the PPC search engine, and the third-party tool.

The function of a third-party tool is solely to carry out certain operations. Because you are paying a fixed fee (either up front via download or in a monthly/yearly arrangement), there is no real incentive for the owners of third-party tools to be anything other than as unbiased as possible.

The same cannot always be said for your search engine, whose purpose is to supply a service, but who also needs to make a profit if it is to continue. Although they may offer you access to tools that have the same functionality as a third-party tool, the advertiser has no way of knowing how those tools were structured or if they are as accurate as they should be.

The Types of Pay-Per-Click Tools Available

There are many different PPC tools available, but they fall into three main categories:

- ◆ Management of your ad campaigns and all associated aspects

- ◆ Keyword generation and/or bidding tools

- ◆ Tracking tools for calculating ROI, detecting possible click fraud, etc.

Of course, some tools overlap these categories and may offer both a bidding tool and a conversion tracker, so it is important to fully check all the features available to ensure you are getting the most robust tool at the lowest cost.

In terms of cost, PPC tools tend to fall into two groups; either they are offered as a piece of software that you download for use or they are offered as a subscription service on a monthly or yearly basis.

It is really up to the individual advertiser to decide which is best for their ad campaign style. Generally speaking, unless you have the time to learn how to use a new piece of software and perhaps even time to maintain the data in the tool itself, most novices will be better off trying a subscriber-based system to begin with.

Many tools offer trial periods or incentives, which can be useful in the assessment process. The goal is to find the tool(s) that will work best for you as an individual and that best fits the way your PPC ad campaign(s) are set up and the amount of data you currently receive from your search engine.

Let's look at 13 of the most popular PPC tools currently available to advertisers and review the service they are offering, their usefulness, pros and cons, and associated costs. Some are simple, one-function tools, but most offer a variety of features.

This is by no means an exhaustive list of the tools available on the marketplace, and new ones are coming online each day, but this should give you a base from which to start investigating some of the more popular options and an opportunity to judge if they may fill your needs.

Pay-Per-Click Management Tools

AdScientist
(www.ppcbook.info/adscientist)

AdScientist is a sophisticated bid management tool that takes all the guesswork out of keyword bidding. Set up your campaign and designate your desired ad positions and maximum bids you wish to pay, and AdScientist will automatically bid to put your ad in the desired position or find the best value position in the range of the maximum amount you wish to bid.

AdScientist has a number of features that can help make your PPC bidding much more competitive. You can specify a range of rankings that you wish to bid to. For example, if you are not too concerned if you rank either second or third, you can set up AdScientist to bid to that range of positions. You can also set up your bidding to change depending upon another URL (a competitor or an affiliate, for example). Some features of AdScientist are not for the faint of heart or the inexperienced. For example, Competitor Killer Mode will manipulate your bidding routine so that your competitors will be under pressure to maintain their ad ranking with a new max bid, after which your bid is immediately lowered to just one cent above that new bid.

The software is tailored towards standard PPC offerings, but a lot of flexibility is available for those advertising in the lands of Google and Yahoo!, which no longer operate in a strict auction format. There is a Google bidding algorithm built in, and the software even has an update incorporating the new Yahoo! Panama ad platform.

With AdScientist, you can manage all your PPC campaigns in one interface. You can synchronize all of your PPC campaigns and use the scheduler to automatically manage them and automatically fund your accounts. Keyword research can be undertaken via the Keyword Builder tool and keywords and ranking results can be easily downloaded. The tool is fully automated and runs in the background.

A Flash demo of the product is available online and a free, 30-day trial is also found on the website. There are three levels of subscription. The Standard level allows 25 accounts and up to 500 keywords for a monthly cost of $27.96 with extra keywords at $10 per month for up to 500 extra keywords. The other two levels—for campaigns up to 5,000 or an unlimited number of keywords—start at $89.96 and $799.96 per month (Professional and Corporate, respectively).

AdScientist is definitely worth consideration. It will make management of your PPC campaigns a lot easier and its up-to-date adaptation to changes in the search engines ensures that your campaigns work with maximum efficiency even when the rules of the game change.

Atlas Search
(www.ppcbook.info/atlas)

Atlas Search (formerly Atlas OnePoint) is a web-based management tool that offers online solutions for many different aspects of online marketing, not just pay per click.

The PPC-related products offered are BidManager and ProfitBuilder, the latter covering ROI tracking and web analytics. BidManager is a robust tool that allows bidding control across almost 30 search engines, which includes major properties as well as a sampling of Yahoo! international sites and MIVA's Espotting branches in various European countries. Results are fed to Atlas, and then BidManager automatically reviews and adjusts your bids across all the engines you have chosen, making strategic bids that help keep you in the same position. You are informed via email of the status of your keyword bids and positions, and these emails can be programmed to arrive as often as each half hour if you desire.

BidManager's Rules-Based Bidding feature lets you customize your bidding to include up to 13 very aggressive variables, including a bidding war component that will apparently deal with "attacks" on your bids. One feature, called Caboose Rule, will move your keyword bid to the minimum allowed by the search engine and then jams the bid above.

ProfitBuilder adds functionality onto ROI, including total visitors, total sales, total cost, average cost per sale, average cost per click, average sale, conversions and conversion percentage, and Return On Advertising Spend (ROAS). You can also look at details of the path visitors took through your site and on shopping cart sessions that were not completed. The analytics provided allow you to sort the data by parameters such as date range, different search engines, different ranks within the PPC ad block, and individual PPC promotions. All of this is extremely powerful and useful information, and it is presented in a clear, easy-to-understand format.

Atlas Search is offered in a Bronze, Silver, or Gold package. The Bronze package includes 600 bid reviews in BidManager (which could be 100 keywords reported 6 times a day or 300 keywords updated 2 times a day) and up to 50,000 page views of ProfitBuilder for $287.44 per month. The Silver package takes the bid reviews up to 3,000 and ProfitBuilder up to 100,000 page views for $739.89 per month. The Gold package is customizable. There is a 14-day free trial so that advertisers can judge whether or not Atlas Search is the right product for their ad campaigns and specific circumstances. It is an extremely robust tool, but you will need to have a fairly large PPC ad campaign setup to justify the monthly charge.

BidRank
(www.ppcbook.info/bidrank)

BidRank is a management tool that has been available for many years from Roffers Engineering in Wisconsin. BidRank is a stand-alone piece of software, so there is no monthly fee, but the user pays for software upgrades.

BidRank is available in two formats. The first, appropriately called "BidRank for Yahoo!," only manages keywords in the Yahoo! PPC environment, not just in the US, but also in a select number of countries in Europe and elsewhere. The second product, "BidRank Plus," supports keyword management in the following search engines: Google AdWords, Searchfeed, Xuppa, Enhance Interactive, Kanoodle, MIVA (FindWhat and Espotting), Mirago, 7Search, Mamma, BrainFox and Que Pasa!

Pricing for each of the products is the same, with a minimum edition and a commerce edition. If an advertiser wishes to use the product with their Yahoo! account as well as a Google account, they must purchase both products. Each is $14.90 per month or $149 per year for 100 keywords to $99.90 per month ($999 per year) for up to 12,000 keywords.

The user may wonder why they would need BidRank, given that Yahoo! Search Marketing itself has various keyword bidding options, including an auto-bidding function. BidRank maintains they go beyond Yahoo! by allowing bidding by rank and gap surfing, while Yahoo! will only auto bid to your maximum amount.

BidRank is a Yahoo!-approved third-party bid-management tool, and allows the user to access the Yahoo! Marketing Console via BidRank itself. Marketing Console is basically an ROI tool and is also offered at various pricing levels, depending upon the number of leads generated. BidRank also offers a toolbar with a link to news and information from BidRank, such as news releases, user tips, upcoming scheduled downtimes, and so on.

Users like BidRank. It has a reputation for excellent customer service, which is very important to people involved in any type of marketing. Aside from its convincing on-site testimonials, their management keeps a close eye on user forums and responds to any complaints they see by implementing changes—a very effective way of keeping customers satisfied.

Directions are clear and the interface is direct and easy to follow. The website itself is quite informative and customer service is quick and efficient. BidRank is on the expensive side, however, so be sure this will work for your particular type and style of ad campaigns before purchase. BidRank offers a 15-day trial offer of a fully functional version of the basic package of up to 100 keywords, with a usage of once every 15 minutes.

IndexTools
(www.ppcbook.info/indextools)

IndexTools is a web analytics offering from TENSA (Technology) Ltd., which has offices in New York and over 200 local "partners" in more than 25 countries. They run an extensive development center in Budapest, Hungary and launched IndexTools Bid Management in 2006 (which is still in beta and available by invitation only at this point).

Their web-analytics setup covers almost every single thing a business owner would like to know about the behavior of visitors to their site—where they came from, the path they took through the site, how long they stayed, and where they went upon leaving the site. Other capabilities include tracking by groups that completed an action such as a sale, or those who arrived to your site via a certain search engine or ad campaign, or the results for two different time periods. You can monitor events such as system outages, public holidays, or website changes to see an analysis of how they affected your website stats. The AskIT™ Tutor will provide an on-screen executive summary of the data when you mouse over a row in an online report—you can copy the summary and use it in your reports.

IndexTools' reports are easy to understand and interactive. Product demos are provided that are also interactive, which makes for a particularly impressive introduction to the product. You can also request a demonstration by one of their Enterprise Client Account Managers if you wish to explore all of the features and reports available.

There are two primary offerings. The Enterprise edition is more customizable, but the E-Business package should be sufficient for most small-to-medium-sized businesses. Both have the ability to exclude certain IP addresses from tracking (so that you do not skew the data with your own employees going about their day-to-day work on your website), tracking within SSL pages, and data reports customizable by timeframe for either CSV or Excel export. The E-Business product is priced at $49.95 for up to 100,000 page views per month. The Enterprise product starts at $249 per month.

IndexTools is ideal for companies doing business both in North America and other parts of the world. IndexTools does not require you to download any software, but you do need to add the JavaScript tracking code to your pages. There is a 15-day free trial of the full-featured version, which lets you see how the product will work for your specific needs.

A good tool, although certainly not a bargain-hunter's option. However, if you are involved in international business, take a look at the trial version and undertake a cost-benefit analysis.

Pay-Per-Click Tracking Tools

Clickalyzer
(www.ppcbook.info/clickalyzer)

Clickalyzer is a traffic analysis tool that specializes in analysis of segments of the traffic to your site. If, for example, you only want to see "visitors that came from Google, spent 5 minutes on my homepage, read half my sales letter, and then purchased on my affiliate website link," Clickalyzer can give you the results you are looking for. This filtering capability is Clickalyzer's main selling point.

The system is centered around eight specific reports—General Statistics, Traffic Evaluation, Visitor Footprints, Traffic Flow Analysis, Webpage Statistics, and three Ad and Search Engine Reports—although reports can be customized.

Special features include Percent Scroll Tracking (which tracks how far down a page the visitor scrolls) and Auto Convert (which allows multi-variable split testing of your ads). With these tools you can identify the specific parts of an individual web page that are working as planned and those which are not converting as you wished.

Clickalyzer allows remote tracking—the ability to track activity on websites that you may promote as an affiliate (or in a similar role) but do not own. The tool, therefore, is useful for affiliates who wish to ensure that their efforts are placed in the sales programs that will bring them the most profit. No code is needed on the "thank you" page.

The on-site demo explains clearly and easily how to use the program. It appears to be fairly intuitive.

There is a 7-day trial of Clickalyzer available for $1 (there appears to be no good reason—other than to obtain your billing information—for this nominal charge).

The product itself is priced at $29.95 month, $299.95 for a year, or $599.95 for a lifetime account. The small print indicates, however, if you have more than 50,000 page views per month "additional service fees" are owed, which turn out to be blocks of page views at a price ranging from 50 cents to $1 per 1,000, depending upon how much your monthly page views are.

Comments that users have made over the last year have been critical of the down time of the Clickalyzer server and the responsiveness of customer service. There have also been observations that the tool only tracks Firefox users. Those considering signing on after the free trial period should be certain to check on these issues.

ConversionRuler
(www.ppcbook.info/conversionruler)

On first glance, ConversionRuler appears to be a fairly typical web analytics tool that concentrates on tracking your ad campaigns and reporting back statistical information on conversions. ConversionRuler is a product of MarketRuler, a company based in Pennsylvania.

ConversionRuler is set up to handle types of advertising other than pay per click, and especially targets email marketing campaigns. This makes it a useful tool for those who are interested in email marketing in addition to pay per click. Its focus on conversions limits its usefulness as a full-featured campaign tracker, but it has a relatively good reputation for conversion tracking.

Although the website has a friendly, casual feel to it, ConversionRuler's description of how to install tracking code into landing pages and "thank you" pages is filled with jargon that novices may find difficult to understand. Their animated "how it works" page is, unfortunately, difficult to follow. Users are, however, encouraged to contact them for assistance if they have difficulty setting up the requisite code on their web pages.

With only a couple of sample report pages available to look at prior to taking their trial or signing up for the software, it is difficult to judge if the level of detail reported will be sufficient and relevant for an individual's needs. Also, the site could benefit from a less "techie" style of writing.

ConversionRuler has improved its offering in many ways over the last year or so, implementing an affiliate program, solidifying the types of reports offered, and, most importantly, improving their stated customer service to be more flexible and accessible.

ConversionRuler offers a 30-day free trial. The pricing of the basic product starts at $19.99 per month, with an additional charge for clickthroughs coming from a "sourced" URL that are over 2,000 for the month.

The "Complete" version starts at $29.99 per month and considers each visitor to the site as a clickthrough (with additional charges for more than 2,000 visitors per month).

The "Cross Tracking" feature is available for $29.99 per month for each additional website.

Even though it may be priced lower than other options, the tool can turn out to be a little overwhelming for those with no programming background or experience.

HyperTracker
(www.ppcbook.info/hypertracker)

HyperTracker bills itself as "the Holy Grail of online marketing," a pretty ambitious claim. Although it's far from the be-all and end-all of marketing tools, it is an easy-to-use tool for analyzing the success of each of your online ad campaigns. Basically, HyperTracker keeps track of the number of unique visitors to each web page and how many sales, clicks, or specified actions are taken and converts that data into ROI information. Its major selling points are its ease of use and security.

HyperTracker, from Implix, works via a generated HTML code that is placed on your website pages. It has been on the market for a number of years and is well-organized and very intuitive. The latest version will even show you which campaigns are going well in the color green and those that are doing poorly in red.

HyperTracker concentrates on testing, an important and vital part of any PPC ad campaign. It is very easy to set up split testing, and the tool is configured to make it easy to compare the results from two different landing pages for a particular campaign. Unfortunately, it doesn't go much further into the actions of visitors on your website, as no tracking outside of actions you have specified takes place (logging information such as browser type, IP address, and some other stats are captured).

Up to 128 target URLs can be set up in your HyperTracker account. If your server can run PHP or Perl, you can eliminate the Hypertracker.com domain name from the redirection link on your web pages. The reports will show you the number of clicks, sales, and actions, as well as your ROI, CPC, and Cost-Per-Sale/Action amounts. You can also set up tracking for different products.

There is a free, two-week trial version available. After that, the cost is $19.95 per month, with discounts available if you sign up for 6 months or a year. The HyperTracker website is a hard-sell type of site with a lot of sales hype and high-action verbiage ("Detonate your website and chop as much as 90% off your marketing expenses …"), but once you get beyond the hype, you will soon discover that the product does have a fair amount to offer. It is easy to use and set up on your website, and customer support is an important part of the equation.

Although it may not have the breadth that some other tracking programs have, for online ad campaigns, HyperTracker can tell you in a clear and easily understood fashion if you are receiving a sufficient number of actions or conversions from your campaigns or not. Its clear reporting on competing ad campaigns is its major advantage. If you want to get down to the bottom line quickly and efficiently, this tool is a good choice.

Click Fraud Monitoring

AdWatcher
(www.ppcbook.info/adwatcher)

AdWatcher's parent company has been in the PPC business for more than 7 years, and has plenty of first-hand experience and knowledge to draw from. AdWatcher is a tracking tool that can analyze any type of ad campaign, with a truly impressive number of tracking features for such an inexpensive tool.

One of AdWatcher's most important strengths is its click fraud monitoring. Traffic is analyzed for suspicious patterns, alerting you to the potential fraud that may be taking place. AdWatcher will notify you via email of potential fraud and will display warning messages to repeat offenders notifying them that the campaign is being monitored. AdWatcher will also help you in your efforts to have click fraud amounts credited back to your PPC accounts with search engines.

The tracking part of the software is extremely precise. It even has an ability to filter duplicate leads/sales and clicks which in turn helps to improve accuracy. There is complete support of all major search engines which makes keyword tracking a breeze. Another great feature is its split-test tracking, something only higher-priced products usually offer.

Customizable email reports are available, which makes it easier for small business owners to always be aware of what's going on. It is coupled with an impressive feature (to our knowledge no other service out there offers anything similar) that allows the user to access their account via a WAP-enabled phone or a PDA anywhere on the road.

For those who do not want to depend on someone else when it comes to click-fraud tracking or for those with large advertising budgets, AdWatcher offers a downloaded version which allows you to install their software on your servers, so you can do everything in-house.

There are multiple options when it comes to customer support including a 24/7 live support, a help desk and a toll-free number. AdWatcher will even help you set up your account and campaign group tracking for free, so that you can begin ad tracking within a few hours. Customer service is a priority for AdWatcher and help is readily available for any problem a user has in either installation or operation.

AdWatcher is offered at only $19.95 per month with a free 30-day trial (and a money-back guarantee). It's a good tool for any small business to help ensure protection from click fraud and help in regaining ad money lost to fraudulent clicks.

Clicklab™
(www.ppcbook.info/clicklab)

Clicklab was founded in 2001 by Dmitri Eroshenko, and offers robust, statistically-based, web analytics with a focus on click fraud detection and prevention. Clicklab is offered either as software or a hosted service and seeks to provide its users with "an understanding of the relationship between traffic, website usability, and revenue." As such, it is customized to each client's specific needs and crafted to fit into your individual sales goals and setup.

Clicklab detects potential click fraud via a scoring algorithm that analyzes actions and assigns a potential "fraud" score to events such as visits from anonymous proxy servers, which would be tagged as a highly suspicious activity. Once the level of such activities reaches a specified point, it is flagged for analysis and action. The process is the end result of over 2 years worth of research and development by a group of mathematicians, programmers and SEM/PPC specialists.

Clicklab will undertake a certified click fraud audit statement, which analyzes the traffic to your website over a period of time in order to estimate the percentage and type of fraudulent traffic you may be receiving from a specific search engine. Although not exactly a cheap option at $200 per search engine, this process could be useful if you suspect a problem with a specific search engine but are having difficulty in making your case to the engine in question. Clicklab analysts will "establish data validity, conduct spot checks, and investigate discrepancies and deviations."

As many web analytics tools are now doing, Clicklab concentrates in its click fraud capabilities, but its wider usage is for full array of web analytics and tracking. What really sets Clicklab apart from the competition is a theory called the ESA/T process, that is a slightly different method of increasing ROI, taking the older idea of Total Quality Management and morphing it into ESA/T (Enhance, Select, Analyze, Test/Tweak).

Clicklab is a very robust, full-featured solution, but not necessarily a low-cost option, especially for smaller businesses.

Monthly costs for click fraud detection start at $300 for up to 20,000 clicks and go all the way up to $5,000 per month for up to 1 million clicks. There is also a $300 setup fee, which covers initial deployment and a reevaluation of the scoring algorithm at the end of 30 days. Pricing for the remaining analytics services vary depending upon your needs.

Click Forensics
(www.ppcbook.info/clickforensics)

Click Forensics has taken a lead in the anti-click-fraud community with the development of the Click Fraud Network and The Click Quality Council, comprised of major advertisers and agencies. The goals of the Council include ensuring that Council members and the 3,000 plus members of the Click Fraud Network are represented in discussions of PPC measurement standards.

Click Forensics is a click fraud detection program for enterprise-sized companies (using a measure of more than 100,000 clicks per month as a rough cut-off point). The company does offer a product for businesses with up to 100,000 clicks per month—CF Analytics—a free product available to any business that signs up to join the Click Fraud Network. Data collected from members of the Network is aggregated and reported as the Click Fraud Index.

CF Analytics provides tracking of potential click fraud only, not other analytics. If you decide to use the free product, remember that by placing the proprietary tagging code on your landing page you will also be agreeing to have statistics from your website included in the database from which the Click Fraud Index is drawn. The company assures that no personal information will be reproduced in any report, just across-the-market data.

A weekly email report gives you an overview of your PPC ad campaigns, and access to online reports is also provided at no charge, as is access to the members-only section of the Click Fraud Network. The focus of the program is to provide you with a "threat" alert level for your PPC campaigns, so that users can assess when and from which sources of traffic they face higher levels of potential fraud. A general overview "threat level" is identified as well as individual data as you drill down in the reports. Threat levels are identified by time of day, search provider, country of origin and week over week.

With somewhere in the neighborhood of 3,000 members, the Click Fraud Network could be a good microcosm of the PPC world, but since its very nature precludes the release of data on the relative size of these sites or which industries they represent, it's impossible to place total certainty on its aggregate statistics until more is known about the make-up of its users.

At this point, CF Analytics (the free tool available if you register in the Click Fraud Network and thereby allow the company access to your stats) may be useful in monitoring click fraud, but it would be prudent to compare results to another tracking system before reaching conclusions on how much click fraud may be affecting your specific site. To its credit, Click Forensics is working hard to remain a neutral party in the highly volatile world of click fraud, and compares itself to Neilsen, Arbitron and other audit services.

ClickDetective
(www.ppcbook.info/clickdetective)

ClickDetective is another relatively new click-fraud detection tool, having come onto the market in January 2005. ClickDetective's features and approach to click fraud are fairly standard, but there are some aspects that set it apart from competitors. Perhaps most importantly, ClickDetective is a UK registered company with offices both in the United States (in Arizona) and in Europe (the UK). An advertiser can contact the US office for North American coverage and the UK office for coverage of ads in Europe and elsewhere.

Another interesting feature of ClickDetective is the ability to customize the level of the alert message that is displayed for daily repeat visitors. You can choose no message, an informational popup for repeat clicks (the threshold is 3 per day) reminding the visitor to bookmark your website for future visits, or a more serious warning that click behavior is being monitored, and an "access denied" message. The text of the messages can also be customized to your preferences.

Your administrative account is immediately sent an email when suspicious behavior is detected so you can choose how to respond upon learning the details. You will also be warned via email if it is anticipated that your paid-for number of clicks will not last through the month.

The reports generated appear fairly basic, but should provide ammunition to take to your PPC search engine. Three basic packages are offered: the CD Standard (at $49 per month, including 2,000 clickthroughs); the CD Corporate (at $79 per month for up to 10,000 clickthroughs); and CD Enterprise (for larger accounts and unlimited numbers of clickthroughs and requires contact with the company). Payment options are in US dollars, UK pounds or Euros—again, providing some needed flexibility for those located outside of the US.

As expected, a free trial is offered. Although it may take up to two days to set up, the trial period only begins when the first clickthrough is sent to ClickDetective. The trial period of 15 days should give you adequate time to determine if ClickDetective adds value to your existing efforts.

ClickDetective's strongest selling point is its European location (in addition to a North American location that is), thus increasing its appeal to companies with international operations. After all, it is bad enough news to discover that a click farm somewhere in the United Kingdom is wreaking havoc with your PPC ad campaigns, without also discovering that your click fraud protection efforts are all located on the wrong (for this situation) side of the Atlantic. ClickDetective removes this concern for companies with overseas operations in the European marketplace.

Keyword Research Tools

Keyword Discovery
(www.ppcbook.info/keyworddiscovery)

Keyword Discovery is an analytical keyword tool offered by Trellian Software (headquartered in Melbourne, Australia) a company that has been a part of the Internet scene since at least 1997. Keyword Discovery was recently revised and enhanced. Their database of keywords is drawn from results of 35 billion searches over the past 12 months (580 million unique search terms).

Over 180 search engines have their data incorporated into the database (including Google, Yahoo!, MSN, and Teoma). The premium database is smaller (about 196 million unique search terms) but is very accurate. Regional databases for the UK and the Netherlands exist and others will be added shortly. There are also shopping search databases, an eBay database, and a news-related database. Keyword Discovery offers the usual and expected keyword-analysis-related functions, such as reporting on how often certain keywords are searched for, providing suggested related keywords for your business, adding misspellings, and coming up with a list of popular search terms for any given keyword.

The Keyword Effectiveness Indicator processes information on both the number of searches for a keyword or phrase and the number of competing sites that use that same word/phrase, and comes up with a 0-10 rating indicating the effectiveness of the word/phrase. The Keyword Density Analysis tool provides a measure of how often a website's keywords are found on a specific web page. The filter tool makes keyword list manipulation a breeze. A cross-reference tool will compare your keywords to those found on competitors' websites.

Keyword Discovery is unique in offering a seasonal search trend report, which can help you see which keywords performed best for certain selling times, such as the holiday season, Valentine's Day, etc. The tool also offers a "related" function, which uncovers keywords with a regional or cultural meaning that may fit your business model. It is most effective using the premium database.

With an excellent online help system and a forum that is kept very up-to-date by the company, there is a free trial that is well worth taking for a spin. A monthly subscription is a relatively hefty $49.95 (or $390 per year). The interface is simple and intuitive and, for the most part, users like this program. Although some of its features are found in free or cheaper tools, its broad database and unique aspects will make it worth the expense, especially if you deal with a lot of keywords in your campaigns.

WordTracker
(www.ppcbook.info/wordtracker)

WordTracker bills itself as "the ultimate tool to increase your website traffic," and in this case, they may be right. Developed in 1999 by Rivergold Associates Ltd., it is definitely a research tool that every PPC advertiser needs to be acquainted with.

At the very least, take advantage of their free trial to see the power behind this product. If you are just beginning to use PPC, the free trial may offer enough to get you started. You can subscribe later, when your campaign needs to be changed. WordTracker is a subscription-based product that specializes in reporting the relative popularity and positioning of keywords. The product provides you with information on keywords related to those you are already using, the number of times any keyword has appeared in their database, and typical misspellings. It also shows how many competing pages exist for your chosen keywords from among the search engines it analyses.

In short, WordTracker is a tool that will help you immensely in choosing keywords that are not only right for your products and services, but are the most advantageous for your particular ad campaign. It is simple to use, yet the information it provides is quick, accurate, and managed extremely well. It takes almost all the guesswork out of which keywords are going to be most effective by showing you what keywords people are using when they search for your type of business.

The website is clean, clear, and attractive. It is filled with information about the product and the company, and offers a quick tour of the features. Although not inexpensive, WordTracker is a tool well worth the expense. A free weekly keyword report shows the top 500 most frequently searched keywords on the Internet, from a database of over 350 million search terms. You can purchase longer lists if you wish, starting at $99 for the top 20,000 keywords. If you are new to the PPC market, or you are running a small campaign, you can subscribe to WordTracker for as short a period as one day for less than $10. For those who are more involved or have larger campaigns, WordTracker subscriptions run weekly, monthly, quarterly, and yearly (maximum cost is about $270).

The company offers a 30-day money-back guarantee, with plenty of research to justify their use of metacrawlers as the basis for their database. Tutorials to help you with keyword selection cater to every level of Internet marketer. WordTracker is definitely the "gold standard" for keyword research for PPC advertising campaigns today.

Conclusion

We trust that the selection of pay-per-click tools we reviewed in this chapter will help you decide to at least experiment with a couple on a trial basis to assess their utility to your individual circumstances.

Tools that help with bid management, choosing keywords that will work best for you, and tracking tools that reveal which of your various campaigns are working better than others, and others like them, are helpful in running a successful ad campaign online.

They can save you both time and money. Their flexibility can automate many of the comparative analytics you would like to see concerning your advertising efforts, but don't have the time to develop. Even though some of the pricing of these tools is quite high, if you find one or more that integrate perfectly with your objectives, you will actually save money in the long run through improved ad performance and a resulting higher ROI.

Their expert assistance, combined with your knowledge of your company's needs, can be the difference between a successful pay-per-click ad campaign and one that just misses the mark.

So far, we've concentrated on aspects of PPC that cost the advertiser money. Now it's time to offer you some insightful and valuable tips from industry experts that you won't find anywhere else. Use these tips to position your PPC ad campaigns for maximum success. Then it is on to an analysis of the trends we see developing in the near future in the paid-search marketplace.

Chapter 12 – Tips From the Experts

We asked a number of experts and top-ranked analysts involved in the field of pay-per-click advertising for their opinions on the industry, as well as their thoughts and tips in the areas of paid advertising they specialize in.

We hope you find these ideas and techniques a helpful addition to managing your PPC ad campaigns.

Andy Beal
Internet Marketing Consultant
www.marketingpilgrim.com

With any search engine marketing campaign, it is vital to understand your customer's typical "buying cycle" and how they make decisions on "what" and "when" to buy from the products or services your company offers. When implementing a pay-per-click campaign, many marketers tend to focus on keyword bid, ad creative and the layout of their landing page, but often forget they need to match the keyword with the appropriate stage in the visitor's buying process.

Depending on the source, there are as many as six or seven stages in a typical buying cycle, but they can be generalized in just three stages: "Research," "Comparison," and "Buying." Depending on the stage a site visitor is in when clicking on your ad, they are either still researching the best product for their needs, comparing features and options, or shopping for the best price. A search marketer can dramatically increase their conversion rate by tailoring their ads to match the intent of the visitor.

My advice for those implementing a paid search campaign is to analyze each keyword bid and place them in one of three buckets—research, comparison or buying. From there, you can better target the ad creative and landing page to match the current state of mind of your visitor. For example, someone clicking on an ad after searching for "desktop computer reviews" is not going to be ready to make a purchase and is likely to leave your site very quickly if you bring them to a landing page that features one product and a shopping cart. Instead, bring that visitor to a page that explains what to look for in a desktop computer, highlights the features of each brand your company offers, and then guides them to a page where they can make a buying decision. You'll win the trust and confidence of the visitor by acknowledging they're not ready to buy, but need assistance in making a decision.

If you take the time to match-up your keyword bids with the likely intent of the customer, you'll see better interaction and higher conversions. And, if you include a good mix of research-type keywords, you'll likely find less competition and the opportunity to convert visitors at a lower cost per click.

Hallie Janssen
Account Director, Anvil Media, Inc.
www.anvilmediainc.com

The long tail of search is only getting longer as searchers are using more and more terms in their search phrases. It is almost impossible to write relevant and compelling ads to alert the searcher that you've got what they are searching for and for the right price. So what do you do when you have a large group of keywords which make it incredibly difficult to write custom ads?

Let's say you have an online computer parts store and you have thousands of products from several manufacturers; and one of your manufacturers is Dell. Of course you have a Dell campaign, and in that campaign you have a Memory Card ad group or order. But how can you customize your ad to capture exactly the various models of memory your searcher is looking for and include customized offers based on that search? Each engine has a slightly different take on ad customization, but we'll review MSN for now.

Remember this doesn't take the place of customizing the rest of your ads and landing pages. The more targeted your message is, the better the ROI. Don't just rely on this tactic alone!

MSN adCenter's Dynamic Text Parameters

MSN adCenter has a different approach to ad customization than Google and Yahoo! They actually offer something very unique by allowing advertisers to create endless versions of ads all in one campaign.

2 Types of Commands: Go to Campaigns > Orders > Keywords > Manage Keywords > Dynamic text and click the Dynamic text link to get a drop-down list of these commands.

{Keyword} inserts a unique keyword from your keyword list into the ad title. As an advertiser, if I have the keyword "dell memory card" in my campaign, then this command will insert that keyword into the title of my ad. However, keep in mind that your ad will be rejected by MSN for any and all keywords that exceed the maximum 25 character limit, so be sure to have a second static ad as a default.

Parameters {Param1}, {Param2}, and {Param3}, allow you to customize the other elements of the ad. Use Param1 when you want to use a keyword-specific tracking string or landing page. Param1 will update each keyword's destination URL. Use Param2 and Param3 when you want to customize the ad text for each keyword. Param2 is commonly used in lieu of the {Keyword} command if the keyword insertion will make the ad title too long. Param3 is commonly used for prices that are updated frequently or for unique pricing per keyword.

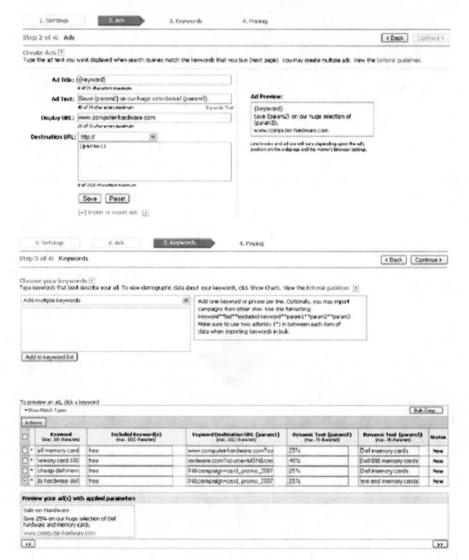

Pierre Zarokian, President
Submit Express, Inc.
www.submitexpress.com

Content ads, such as those like Google AdSense, allow website owners to place ads on their site and therefore share revenue with the site owners. For this reason, there is more click fraud with CPC content advertising than CPC search advertising. Our statistics also show that content ads do not have as good an ROI as search advertising for most sites, whether due to click fraud or the content ads serving on low-quality sites.

My recommendation is to turn off the content serving ads completely or to bid about 1/3 of what you would normally bid on a keyword. This is especially important for high-value terms (over $1.00 per click). Generally, the higher the value, the more click fraud there is.

Kevin Gold, Co-Founder
Enhanced Concepts, Inc.
www.enhancedconcepts.com

I have managed over 200 pay-per-click campaigns for clients in diverse markets with varying objectives, including lead generation and first-time product sales. All of my engagements have been performance-driven versus brand-oriented, meaning that the client expected a net ROI. Therefore, traffic volume was secondary to generating positive financial results—strong net margins. As such, I focus intensely on performance and my strategies reflect this. Here are two primary ones for performance-driven pay-per-click management:

Keyword-level tracking using exact matches versus broad or phrase. It takes more effort, but the results are significant. By measuring actions of sales or leads at the exact keyword-level (or as I refer to it, "the root"), a data-driven decision is made to maximize, adjust, or drop the keyword, based on its individual performance.

The surge in website conversion comes from continuously driving at greater consistency and relevancy from the user's selected keyword to your paid ad to your landing page. The greater the consistency and relevancy to the user's preconceived expectation, the higher the probability of the user acting on your call-to-action. This means utilizing custom landing pages and testing, via A/B splits, different landing pages for greater consistency and relevancy. By connecting your message with the user and "pulling" them through your ad to your landing page, you are in essence getting the user to say "yes" multiple times, while your strong and clear call-to-action on the landing page "asks for the close"—just like a traditional salesperson.

Nancy Houtz
PayPerClick4U.com
www.payperclick4u.com

One of my best strategies is to keep thinking "outside the box." This includes how I bid, bid amounts, keywords to use, and even the descriptions. Example: think like potential buyers. What ad would motivate and sell? What sets your service/product apart from the herd? What are other competitors not doing that you can do?

With Google, it pays to set different maximum bids within the same ad group, instead of just one maximum bid for the group. Sometimes I even set a keyword lower than the ad group maximum bid. Google sets your position based on a variety of factors, including clickthrough rates, ad group maximum bid, and daily budget. My strategy is always to try to out-think them on this and find the winning combination for maximum position.

Conversion counting is very helpful. It works best if you track the individual keywords receiving conversions over time to figure out trends. Why some conversions and not others? Once figured out, making appropriate adjustments can save on costs. Both Google and Yahoo! Search Marketing offer Conversion Counting for free and have a fairly simple set-up process.

With very high-volume keywords, I've found it doesn't pay to be in first position if the product and prices are competitive. Searchers will usually click on the first ad and work their way down the list, often forgetting to come back up. Wasted click.

Hollis Thomases, President & CEO
Web Ad.vantage, Inc.
www.webadvantage.net

According to a July 2006 Nielsen NetRating, 49.2% of all Internet searches happen on Google. We thought we'd share a few of our agency's best tricks for getting the most return on your AdWords campaigns.

1. Set up a granular campaign
Google accounts can have 25 campaigns with up to 100 ad groups per campaign so don't just throw all your keywords into one campaign. Setting up granular campaigns and ad groups provides more detailed keyword performance data and helps you target your keywords and ad copy more effectively.

2. Use Ad Group Variations

Don't forget that you can run more than one ad per ad group. In fact, you can run up to 50 ad variations at one time. Set up your campaign with several ads so that you can test them over time to see which ones are performing the best.

3. Keyword Insertion Increases CTR

{KeyWord:Default Ad Copy} Does this code mean anything to you? It's an easy trick to implement when writing Google ad copy that studies have shown increases CTR (clickthrough rate.) Keyword Insertion is a small bit of code that you can put in the title or the description of your ad. When a user searches for a term that you are bidding on, or a variation on that term, the actual user-entered keyword will appear in your ad. It's a great way to customize your ad per searcher.

4. Negative Keywords

Negative keywords are used to filter out certain keywords that people are typing in that aren't relevant, but are triggering your keywords. Negative keywords need to be used in conjunction with your existing keywords for the best results. In addition, negative keywords can have a broad, phrase, or exact match applied, so use these accordingly.

5. Google Trends

Recall those millions of people who search on Google every day? Google Trends allows you to compare and contrast keywords according to search volume, top search regions, top search cities, and top languages. It's a great tool for analyzing new PPC keywords or understanding your existing ones.

Jay Lipe, President
Emerge Marketing, LLC
www.emergemarketing.com

Pay-per-click campaigns, like all other marketing campaigns, are perpetual works in progress. The following tips will help you successfully manage your PPC campaign, after you launch.

Study your reports—It can't be said enough—track your bidding results frequently. At a minimum you should analyze your tracking reports weekly. In today's PPC game, with costs rising faster than a kite on a windy day, you must proactively analyze your bidding results.

Choose either traffic or conversions—If you're spending boatloads of money to generate traffic, bravo. But is this traffic converting? That's the real goal. Find a way to track conversions of your PPC traffic (not so easy, I know), and that will help you prioritize your keywords. If you're serious about generating conversions, then you must look at your keywords through that prism.

Prioritize terms by their place in the buying cycle—Searchers will use one set of keywords (e.g., "review" or "compare") to find information, and an entirely different set (e.g., "buy") to find an item to purchase.

If your site is targeted towards the casual searcher (e.g., a review site) then research keywords make sense. But if you want qualified buyers that are hot-to-trot, focus more on buying keywords. The real art of PPC is striking a delicate balance between these two types of words, and your budget.

Circle back with your customers—You already know that a key resource for generating keywords is your customer base. If you didn't ask your customer base for help identifying keywords before your PPC launch, now is the time. Call or email 10 of your customers and ask them this question:

If you were searching for a business (or product, or service) like ours, which terms would you key in? Don't be surprised if this exercise generates a couple of keywords you overlooked before launching.

Jettison well-known branded terms—If you've bid on recognizable branded terms (e.g., your company name or its products), save your money. Your site should be well-optimized for these brand names already, so why pay money for these clicks? Instead, spend your money on non-branded terms and let your company's natural SEO speak for your brand.

Use Google Alerts as an analytical tool—Google Alerts is a wonderful, free service that sends you email alerts whenever there are new Google results for search terms that you've specified. You can use Google Alerts to monitor products (I use it to monitor mentions of my books "The Marketing Toolkit for Growing Businesses" and "Stand Out from the Crowd") and competitors. But it can also be used to monitor certain keyword phrases that you are interested in. Go to http://www.google.com/alerts to sign up for this free service.

Chris Richardson, Search Engine Writer
WebProNews
www.webpronews.com

Consider smaller, more niche-related search engines to display your ads in. Don't limit yourself to AdWords and Yahoo! Search Marketing. Business-to-business engines can have conversion rates as high as 8%. Most general-purpose search engines average 1%-2%.

Keyword monitoring is absolutely imperative. Knowing what people are actually searching for is good practice when considering a PPC campaign. Know how well your target keywords perform in search engines. Meaning: be knowledgeable of whether people are searching for what you are offering and adjust accordingly.

Any gift-based holiday season is a good time to capitalize on PPC campaigns, especially for consumer goods that could be considered gift-worthy. Boosting your bid amount and optimizing keywords are effective methods for those attempting to capitalize on holiday spending.

Don't limit your ads to merely search engines. The Google AdSense program has many different areas PPC ads can appear in. Search engine results are just one area. Google ads can appear on websites, emails, and blogs. Yahoo allows Yahoo! Search Marketing members to display ads in the MyYahoo! RSS feed reader.

Perry Marshall, Google AdWords Expert
Perry S. Marshall & Associates
www.perrymarshall.com

Ultimately, buying web traffic reduces a complex process to a simple question: "How much can you afford to pay for a visitor and still make a profit?" At first, you don't know how many visitors you need to make a sale. To find out—fast—buy traffic and test it.

Here's a checklist to improve visitor value:

- Does your web page have: (1) an attention-getting, benefit-driven headline, (2) a statement of unique value, (3) an offer, (4) a definite call to action, and (5) an easy way to respond?

- Can you improve the headline? This determines whether the person continues to read or not.

- Does page one offer something specific? Visitors need a simple, clearly written page that tells them what they'll get if they respond today.

- What are you offering to test response? Simply by changing the payment terms, including a bonus gift, or adding a gift-wrap option, you could double your sales.

♦ Can visitors opt-in and give you their name and email address? Also get their postal address, phone, and fax number. Reward them with a free gift. If you do a good job asking for an opt-in, you can get a 5%-40% response, and a chance to sell to them later.

1. Research bid prices: check Yahoo! Search Marketing to see advertisers' top bids, then see Google to learn what bidders are paying for top slots.

2. Use Yahoo! Search Marketing and Google to scope out the competition: see how many searches your product gets and how many competitors there are.

3. Extend this search to related keywords, using the Yahoo! Search Marketing Inventory Tool and WordTracker.

4. Break your campaign down into narrow groups of keywords: include different names for your product, abbreviations, or acronyms ("customer relationship management software," "crm software," etc.).

5. Create individual ad groups for related keywords. Each of these is a narrow "silo" that you can match to an ad and know exactly what customers are searching for.

6. Start by writing at least two different ads. In each, the first line shows the product you are advertising. The second line gives a benefit—what prospects actually want. The third line gives a feature—what prospects get when they come to your site. The fourth line shows your display URL—a real page on your site. The last line is the actual destination or landing page.

7. For your destination page, enter a specific page on your site that has a free download offer related to your keywords.

8. Now add your keywords for each ad. Put quotes and brackets around them, so you have three versions of each: broad match, "phrase match," and [exact match].

9. Add negative keywords ("-free crm software") to screen out keywords or phrases you don't want. Be careful not to negate positive keywords (for example, "-software").

10. Don't take the Google suggested bid price. Bid a lower price and see what slots are projected: lower positions generally convert better to sales.

11. Don't rely exclusively on the Google Daily Budget Tool. Deal with budgets by adjusting bid prices.

The first list of keywords you come up with, even if it's a long one, will always be incomplete. People search for all kinds of things and you never know all they are going to hunt for at first.

Aside from the many tools that generate keywords (Yahoo! Search Marketing, WordTracker and others), you have a host of options:

1. Brainstorm for synonyms, related terms, and related subjects.

2. Consider bidding on brand names (caution: legal issues may be involved here). Names of companies and celebrities may relate to your product.

3. Bid on misspellings. Most advertisers don't, and the click-thru rate is higher. I've seen Tolkein (misspelled) get twice the CTR of Tolkien (spelled correctly).

4. www.lexfn.com is an extremely useful website. It's a thesaurus using web technology to generate synonyms and related concepts.

5. Google Keywords Suggestion tool is useful and has recently been improved, but it's still just a starting point.

6. For each keyword, add variations:

   o Nouns: add plurals (shoe, shoes)

   o Verbs: add tenses (drive, drove, driven, driving)

   o Hyphenation: add terms with/without hyphens or spaces (email, e-mail, e mail)

   o Names: use initials with/without periods, or full names (Tolkien, JRR Tolkien, J.R.R. Tolkien, John Ronald Reuel Tolkien)

   o Adjectives: add as applicable!

   o Apostrophes: add correct and incorrect versions (driver's, drivers')

   o Acronyms: add complete term, with/without periods, spelled out (CIA, C.I.A., Central Intelligence Agency)

7. Domain Names: People frequently type domain names into Google

8. Glossaries and Indexes: if you have a book on the product or topic you're advertising, check these sections for ideas

9. Geography: sometimes places are associated with business—for example, clicks may be cheaper for "Niagara Falls" than "Casino"

10. Local businesses: add your state, city, and surrounding cities to the keywords for your business

John Slade, Senior Director
Yahoo! Search Marketing
www.searchmarketing.yahoo.com

Properly targeting your sponsored search titles and descriptions is vital to the success of your campaigns. The more precise the information, the easier it is for your customers to determine if your website will be able to meet their needs. Here are some rules to remember:

Include the keyword in the title and description. Research shows users were nearly 50% more likely to click on listings in which the keyword was included in both the title and description.

Write titles and descriptions that are tailored, clear, and factual. Avoid superlatives (i.e., excessive or exaggerated language, such as "best," "largest," or "cheapest"). Accurately describe what users will find when they go to your site. Again, research shows users were over 50% more likely to click on listings with a factual title and description versus a "salesy" listing.

Avoid ampersands (&) and numbers replacing words ("buy 1 get 2 free"). These types of short cuts seem to have a negative impact on likelihood to click and perceived quality.

When the geographic location is relevant, include it in the description. Including the location will help users determine whether or not your site fulfills their needs, resulting in more qualified leads to your site and fewer wasted clicks.

Landing Pages. Many search marketers understand how important it is to research keyword lists and write effective titles and descriptions, but then overlook one of the most vital steps in creating positive results—choosing the correct landing page. In order to maximize conversions, you must link the user to the most clear and obvious path to the product they are searching for. For instance, if a user clicks on a listing for a "green V-neck sweater" and is delivered to a generic home page, that user then has to start their search all over again. We all know how frustrating this can be.

Instead, link the user directly to the page displaying all of the "green V-neck sweaters" you have for sale on your website. For more general terms like "gift," link the user to a gift guide that allows them to refine what they are looking for. The closer you can get the user to their desired product or service on the first try, the higher your conversion rates will be.

Michael Nguyen, SEO Strategist
Shopzilla, Inc.
www.shopzilla.com

Mine your own logs for keywords. Site search data and natural search referrals are both good keyword sources that can be imported into your PPC campaigns.

Utilize a central keyword database. Use this to store all keyword level data—PPC keywords, SEO keywords, site search keywords, page categories, social media tags, products, etc.

Automate as much as you can, and not just bid management. Think about automating keyword discovery, keyword expansion, bid management, localization, inventory, ad copy, landing page testing and competitive intelligence.

Tie all these steps into your web analytics data to get a feedback system that optimizes itself.

For example, your system can mine your logs for geo-specific data and convert that data into localization keywords (zip codes, cities, neighborhoods, etc.) and combine these keywords with your current list.

These new keywords are then used to create dynamic ad copy and landing pages that are tested and analyzed. Winners are kept and used to generate more keywords, while losers are dropped.

Piggyback. Many of your PPC competitors may offer PPC advertising of their own and allow you to purchase ads on their landing pages. By promoting your products across multiple PPC listings, you improve the chance that a searcher will buy from you.

Continually test everything. Every keyword, ad copy, and landing page needs to be tested to determine exactly how much profit/cost it brings to your business.

Continually testing will help you to improve on your campaigns and maximize profit. Test on the most granular level that your systems are capable of analyzing.

Jaan Kanellis, a.k.a. IncredibleHelp
KBK Marketing
www.kbkmarketing.com

Start Small in PPC

I see this more often than not. When the average PPC campaign starts they throw a thousand keywords into the mix. Man, that is a lot to watch if you want this campaign to make money! Instead start small. Start with sections of your website. Each section can be a mini-campaign on its own. This will allow you to ensure, one by one, that each section is operating at an ideal conversion rate.

Know Your Keywords

Sure, this has been said a million times by most marketers, but it is one of the most important steps in succeeding in PPC. Make sure the keywords you purchase are the ones that are making your PPC campaign money. Don't simply buy keywords just because you think they are relevant to your campaign. One of the first things I usually do when taking over campaigns is to "cut the fat" by removing keywords that are relevant, but simply not converting. Understand that there are likely other reasons for a keyword to not convert. These need to be investigated before removing it from your campaign. These include bid rate, ad copy, and landing page to name a few.

AB Testing

If you're not doing this, start now. Everyone wants to think they have the best copy or landing page, but from my experience, using spilt or AB testing teaches you the most about your visitor. AB testing is nothing new to marketers, but many of those that have PPC accounts rarely use it. Yes, this takes time if you are a small business, but what you learn will not only help you make your PPC campaign more money than ever, it will also improve the overall usability of your website for the average visitor.

You're Not Alone

You should always take anything you read online about PPC and SEM now-a-days with a grain of salt. There is simply too much disinformation out there now without researching and fact-checking sources before taking their advice on anything. With that being said, you should get out there and find a forum/website you are comfortable with so when you do have questions on anything PPC related, you can find the help you are looking for.

Edward Cowell, Technical Director
Neutralize (**)
www.neutralize.com

Screen Resolution. Exploring deeper into position optimizing, one should consider the average user's screen resolution:

1280 x 1024   1024 x 768

With a screen resolution of 1280 x 1024, on a Google search, the user is able to see eight sponsored ads. However, on a more conventional screen resolution, 1024 x 768, the user is only able to see four to five ads.

Hence to appear "above the fold" you need to be bidding high enough to rank at or above position four.

Ad Positioning Across Search Engines. Running a pay-per-click campaign across multiple search engines offers some interesting strategic decisions regarding ad placement on the SERP. Where to rank in a bid landscape is evidently more complex than simply ranking as high as possible.

Debates remain on the subject of which positions drive the best traffic. By carrying out some bid rank analysis on your conversions, one can analyze correlations between the two, spotting trends that appear where more conversions occur at one position over another.

Evident to us, however, is the organizational layout of the search engine results pages themselves. Whilst Google AdWords display eight or more sponsored listings per page, the Yahoo! Search Marketing network of search engines can display anywhere from 5 to 15 listings. Therefore, vying for position 6 would mean that your ad is not seen within the first page of results on some search pages. Thus, depending on CPCs always ranking in position 1–5 on a Yahoo! partnered site may well be beneficial to your campaign.

It is good to consider in which location your ads will appear across the pay-per-click search engine's primary distribution partners. Based on standard top, side, and bottom placement policy for most search engines, the SERPs will be organized as follows, which means your ads will be displayed on the following SERPs in the locations indicated, depending on which position you bid for.

Google		Yahoo		MSN	
Ad	**Position**	**Ad**	**Position**	**Ad**	**Position**
1	Side	1	Top	1	Top
2	Side	2	Top	2	Top
3	Side	3	Top	3	Top
4	Side	4	Yahoo Ad	4	Side
5	Side	5	Side	5	Side
6	Side	6	Side	6	Side
7	Side	7	Side	7	Side
8	Side	8	Side	8	Side
9	Next Page	9	Side	9	Bottom
10	Next Page	10	Side	10	Bottom
11	Next Page	11	Side	11	Bottom
12	Next Page	12	Side	12	-----
13	Next Page	13	Side	13	-----
14	Next Page	14	Bottom	14	-----
15	Next Page	15	Bottom	15	-----

Search engine page layouts vary greatly. We are often limited as to the amount of text we can write within an advertisement. For example, MSN listings contain abbreviated Yahoo! Search Marketing sponsored ads on the right side of the page, but full-length ads at the top.

Truncated ads are limited to 70 characters, whereby the ads across the top have a greater length of 125 characters. The ideal scenario would be to write your ad so that it appears clearly and unabbreviated for each position.

This is achievable by creating the ad in two sentences with the first sentence ending precisely at 70 characters. For example, "Promote your company online. Search engine optimization by Neutralize. Search engine marketing and optimization experts."

Thus the ad will appear unabbreviated on the right side:

SPONSORED SITES

Search Engine Marketing
Promote your company online.
Search engine optimisation by
Neutralize...
www.neutralize.com

Then, if you position your ad at the top of the page, you achieve an increased ad length and are able to display more of your message:

Search Engine Marketing - www.neutralize.com
Promote your company online. Search engine optimisation by Neutralize. Search marketing and optimisation experts.

Calculating truncation points gives you the maximum possibility to present effective messaging toward your target audience.

**Cindy McMahen
Search Marketing Pros, Inc.
www.searchmarketingpros.com**

The book "The 22 Immutable Laws of Marketing," by Al Ries and Jack Trout, is one of my favorites. As a pay-per-click advertiser, it's the 5th Law of Focus that "the most powerful concept in marketing is owning a word in the prospect's mind." For example, when you hear the word "overnight," you think of Federal Express.

This law challenges us, as marketers, to boil our message down to just one idea; or in this case, one word. The lesson being that if you can teach your market segment to associate you with a single idea, perhaps even a single word, you can be a market leader.

When I read the above law, I started reflecting on my clients who have been most successful in the pay-per-click and search-engine-optimization (SEO) arena. Often they wanted to "own" a particular phrase; but they also purchased many, many additional keywords surrounding their products and offerings.

It's a wise strategy. While general keywords (the ones you want to "own") may generate a lot of visitors to your website and help brand you in the prospect's mind, highly targeted and specific keywords are more likely to be used by people who have done their research and are now ready to buy. After all, the primary goal of any pay-per-click campaign is not just to get visitors or drive traffic to your site, but to get visitors who will convert into a sale or lead.

Building Keyword Inventory. I'm often asked by clients how to get a good list of keywords for their pay-per-click campaigns. Here's a list of suggestions to start with in building up your own keyword inventory:

1. **Find a general keyword and add or expand on it**—Try a yellow page search, Yahoo! Directory, or <u>DMOZ.org</u> search to get some basic classifications and keywords down. Google AdWords has a keyword suggestion form that is useful in coming up with general and similar keywords for beginning your quest.

2. **After you flesh out 5-10 primary keywords to build from, consider whether or not your site's content and existing pages are developed around any of these primary keywords**—Because you're going to have to refer people to some part of your site related to their query, you need to know from the start if you'll be able to direct them to existing pages, or if new content, product pages, or landing pages need to be created. It's been stated that, on average, 25% of keyword submissions to Yahoo! Search Marketing fail to get accepted, so to get your keywords past the editors you'll want to become familiar with each search engine's listing guidelines. Put simply, the relevancy requirements in most PPC engines are such that the site and page content that the listings refer to must clearly and obviously reflect the search term in order to qualify it.

3. **Take primary keywords and add specific words to each**—Consider different keyword combinations around these 5–10 primary keywords. Two tools we recommend are the Yahoo! Search Marketing Search Term Suggestion Tool and the Wordtracker Keyword Universe tool. You simply put in a keyword and are provided with many different

additional keyword combinations stemming from it as well as some indicators of popularity. Many PPC engines also offer keyword suggestions to advertisers to use in their administration areas.

4. **Review your competitors' site pages and pay-per-click buys for additional keywords**—Look at the keywords in their titles, descriptions and HTML source code (i.e., keyword meta tags) at their sites, as well as in their advertising.

5. **Look for stats pages containing information on traffic delivered to competing sites**—Dan Thies, author of the ebook "Search Engine Optimization Fast Start," offers this suggestion. He says it's often possible to come up with competing websites who have erroneously forgotten to password protect their stats, and they can be readily found through the search engines. I myself have stumbled on a number of them, and thanks to his ebook know how to look for more.

6. **Review your site's visitor statistics and search engine referral information for keywords**—Your logs are a goldmine just waiting for you as far as potential keywords you can bid for. Reports available through Inktomi inclusion programs will also yield some information on phrases that visitors found you through.

7. **Lastly, start thinking like one of your customers**—Consider asking your customers or others outside of your business what they would type into a search engine. Look at whether they are more commonly using singular or plural forms, may be including brand names, or geographic (location-specific) terms in their queries.

Peter Da Vanzo
Search Marketing Consultant
www.searchengineblog.com

Finding it difficult to get clicks? Are your bid prices sky-high and you're still not getting on the first page of results?

Now that paid-click search marketing is maturing, much of the low-hanging fruit has been gobbled up. Prices are rising and many keyword areas are now highly competitive. One way to increase your chances of getting clicks, without bidding over your budget, is to go wide in your keyword niche. Dig out obscure keyword terms and use them in your campaigns. If you haven't done so already, I recommend that you become familiar with the concept of the Long Tail. Here's a good place to start: http://longtail.typepad.com/the_long_tail/.

In essence, The Long Tail, when applied to search marketing, means there may be just as much traffic, if not more traffic, for the (low-priced) minor terms collectively, than for the (high-priced) popular terms. All those single clicks on obscure keyword terms can really add up.

So, how do you apply the long tail concept? Doesn't everyone use a wide range of keywords?

Yes, they do. However, people are often lazy. They use the keyword tools and cut and paste lists. What many overlook is that these keyword tools are popular; so many other marketers will be using the same keyword lists in their campaigns.

In order to get a jump on your competitors, you should trawl through your site logs looking for organic search engine referral terms. Use those terms in your PPC campaign. Publish as many pages as you can on your site, and use them to mine keyword data from the organic listings. If you see a few referrals for an obscure term, post an article on the same topic, and use those words and phrases. Then watch what other referrals this page catches. Incorporate these terms into your PPC campaign. Repeat the process.

Also, use associations. Incorporate dates, prices, and geographic regions into your keyword list, as appropriate. Use competitor names (if possible), use event names, book titles, the names of television programs, etc.

Keep tracking the data. Run with the winners and cut the losers. Research. Repeat.

___

Troy Lerner
Senior Manager, Business Development
Avenue A | Razorfish Search
www.ar-search.com

Predicting Traffic and Conversions in Pay-Per-Click Advertising. One of the biggest challenges in pay-per-click advertising is knowing what kind of traffic to expect, and what rank to target for your listings. As you do keyword research, various advertising channels and third party toolsets will provide you with a breakdown of total search volume for relevant key phrases. This search volume generally represents the total number of searches per month for the key phrase, not the number of times your ad will appear, and most certainly not the number of visitors you can expect to your site. In addition, you will likely choose not to be in position one for some or all of your listings, impacting your traffic potential even more.

Predicting Clicks. The number of clicks you will receive from keyword searches is based on two primary factors: impressions and click-through-rate (CTR). Impressions indicate the number of times your ad appears, and CTR represents the percentage of clicks you receive versus the number of impressions you receive.

Below is a table illustrating aggregated statistics for impressions and CTR by rank.

The fourth column, "Per 1000," shows the number of clicks you can expect per 1000 monthly searches for a given key phrase. Note that your title and description can have considerable impact on your CTR, and CTR varies by industry, but these factors should not diminish the overall trend of a decrease in CTR in accordance with a decrease in rank.

Rank	Impressions	CTR	Per 1000
1	100%	9.3%	93.0
2	90%	4.1%	37.0
3	90%	1.4%	12.6
4	76%	2.0%	15.3
5	65%	1.4%	9.1
6	47%	1.9%	9.0
7	28%	0.9%	2.5
8	21%	0.9%	1.9
9	38%	2.2%	8.3
10	21%	0.9%	1.9

Predicting Conversions. One additional factor should be considered as you model the potential of your pay-per-click advertising: conversion rate. If conversion rate were consistent across all ranks, it could be disregarded for this analysis, but conversion rate does vary with position. The specific conversion rates indicated here are based on an overall conversion rate of 2%. The "Variance" column indicates variance from the 2% rate.

To calculate rates based on a different overall rate, multiply the base rate by the variance. For example, changing the base rate to 3% would result in a 1st rank rate of 3% x 121%, or 3.6%. The fourth column, "Per 1000," indicates the number of conversions to be expected per 1000 monthly searches.

The fourth column is obtained by multiplying the fourth column of the previous Predicting Clicks chart by the conversion rate.

Rank	Conversion %	Variance	Per 1000
1	2.42%	121%	1.62
2	1.89%	94.3%	0.50
3	1.75%	87.5%	0.16
4	1.78%	89.2%	0.20
5	2.00%	100.0%	0.13
6	2.46%	122.8%	0.16
7	1.83%	91.6%	0.03
8	2.11%	105.5%	0.03
9	2.15%	107.7%	0.13
10	2.06%	102.8%	0.03

About the Data. The data used to generate these statistics has been aggregated from a variety of sources, representing a wide variety of industries, sizes of company and types of products and/or services. The data reflects a proportionate sampling of several of the major pay-per-click advertising channels. While the numbers here may be useful for benchmarking purposes, it is strongly recommended that you establish your own metrics based on data specific to your business and online marketing strategy.

Where to go from here? To truly leverage the power of the data presented here, you will need to build comparable tables based on real statistics obtained by your business, and associate them with bid landscape data for your terms. Tables like these, populated with data accurate to your business, can form the cornerstone of a campaign modeling methodology that will allow you to experiment with scenarios designed to optimize profits or sales, or find the best balance in between.

Actionable Data: How much ROI data is enough to be useful? In the past several years, Internet marketing ROI tracking solutions have proliferated, and most ad channels now offer some form of ROI tracking. Chances are, you are faced with a wide variety of reports telling you about your impressions, clicks and buys. If so, you may well have asked the question, "How much data do I need to start making decisions?" If you haven't asked that question, you should, as the amount of data you receive regarding a particular campaign or ad has a direct bearing on the profitability and sales volume of your online business.

An Example. We will use a paid search listing for this example, but the principles apply to banner, email, affiliate, and other marketing channels as well.

Let's say that you average 2% conversion on visits-to-buys on your website. For a particular search listing, you receive 100 clicks and one buy in a month's time. Common sense tells you that you should have received two buys in that 100 clicks, so therefore you bid the listing down. While this may have been the right thing to do, an analysis of the probabilities involved tells us that due to random variation, there is a better than 40% chance that you will receive zero or one buy on 100 clicks, assuming a 2% conversion rate! In addition, there is a 32% chance you will receive three or more buys, once again assuming a 2% conversion rate. Therefore, using this amount of ROI data to manage bids could lead you to bid incorrectly more than 72% of the time!

Accuracy of Prediction Based on Various Click Volumes. The chart below shows the probability distribution of predicted ranges of conversion rate for various sample sizes (#'s of clicks), assuming an actual 2% conversion rate.

	Sample Size (# of Visitors)						
	100	**200**	**300**	**400**	**500**	**1000**	**5000**
< 0.8%	13.3%	08.9%	06.0%	01.3%	01.0%	00.0%	00.0%
0.8-1.6%	27.1%	34.2%	22.2%	29.8%	20.8%	15.3%	01.7%
1.6-2.4%	27.3%	19.7%	46.3%	40.7%	57.8%	69.2%	96.2%
2.4-3.2%	18.2%	26.3%	17.3%	22.0%	18.1%	15.0%	02.2%
>3.2%	14.1%	10.8%	08.2%	06.2%	02.6%	00.4%	00.0%

Note that because of the discrete nature of conversion events, and due to the arbitrarily discrete selections of conversion ranges and sample ranges, the data appears irregular, or "lumpy." In practice, it is always safe to say that a larger sample will provide a more accurate estimate of probability.

How to read this chart: The percentages indicate probability that the data will predict a conversion rate within the range indicated in the left-most column. For example, given a sample size of 300, random variations in the data will predict a 0.8-1.6% conversion rate 22.2% of the time. The middle range, 1.6-2.4%, is the most accurate range, because the actual conversion rate is 2.0%. Conversion percentages have been represented as ranges to simplify the presentation.

What does this mean? It means that if we use the data alone to ascertain conversion rate, we will need a fair amount of data to do so accurately. If you are not familiar with this kind of analysis, think of flipping a coin.

If you flip a coin twice, there is an equal chance of achieving each of the four following outcomes: heads and heads; heads and tails; tails and heads; tails and tails. Therefore, if you don't know anything about coins, and use the data from a two-flip trial to ascertain probabilities, there is a 25% chance that you will determine that a particular coin always lands on heads, a 50% chance that you will determine that it falls 50/50 heads and tails, and a 25% chance that you will determine that it always lands on tails.

As a point of reference, this could be represented in a chart similar to this:

Sample Size (# of Flips)	
2	
Always Heads	25.0%
50/50 Heads and Tails	50.0%
Always Tails	25.0%

Note that the smaller the probability of an event, the larger the sample you will need to accurately predict the future probability of the event. Keep this in mind when you think about analyzing banner, email or incentive promotions, which typically fall well below average site conversion.

What does this tell us? This tells us that we need to use ROI data with caution, and if you don't focus on conversion rate when you analyze your ROI data, don't think that you are safe! Commonly used factors such as CPA, CPS and ROAS are directly related to conversion rate. In fact, any metric relating to ROI will necessarily be impacted by these same principles. Several useful lessons can be learned from the data above:

- You will need to analyze (at least) thousands of clicks to reasonably estimate the performance of an ad.

- Far fewer clicks may be sufficient to identify exceptionally well or poor performing ads. For example, looking at the previous data tells us that given a sample size of 500 and an overall conversion rate of 2%, random variation will result in a less than 0.8% predicted conversion rate 1% of the time. This can be equated to three or fewer sales. Therefore, if you get three or fewer sales in 500 clicks for an ad, you can be 99% sure that the ad is under-performing your overall conversion rate.

♦ By classifying groups of ads, you can aggregate results to achieve the minimum data necessary to reasonably assess performance. The most effective method for doing so will vary by ad channel and industry.

Where to go from here? If you are using ROI tracking data to inform your advertising and marketing decisions, you should develop a set of guidelines that tell you what amount of data is necessary to reliably make and/or influence decisions.

Eric Layland, Search Marketing Director
Point It!
www.pointit.com

1. This sounds simplistic, but "have a clue" when starting your program. Outline your objectives and how measured success will be determined. Doing so will be your baseline. You must take the perspective that PPC is one component of your larger online marketing agenda. Your site's appearance, performance, and user experience on through to the desired action must all support each other. There's no better example of the concept "garbage-in, garbage-out" than PPC programs. Test, refine, and test more, with regularity and stated objectives and expectations.

2. For lead generation programs, don't try to sell a product on the landing page! Engage the visitor and start a dialog. A website isn't going to effectively convert prospects to a sale of a product or service that's highly considered. Human interaction shouldn't be underestimated. Use copy and calls-to-action to get visitors interested in taking the next step (e.g. download white paper, request demo, contact by company). The offer of free information is great, but shouldn't be over-used. Develop your site into a marketing machine by engaging with the prospect, offering appropriate information, and collecting what's needed to further the sales process.

3. Programs that are generating leads which are passed to a sales team for closing must require sales personnel to identify the source of leads. Ignoring this simple step undermines the effectiveness of the PPC program when it comes to determining revenue generated for products with long sales cycles.

Eli Feldblum, Director of Marketing
Did-it.com Search Marketing
www.did-it.com

Contrary to popular belief, local search isn't just for local advertisers. If you have a product or service that works on a local and national scale, consider running a couple of local PPC campaigns instead of, or in addition to, a national campaign. Your ads will appear more targeted, especially if they specify the location in the ad, and will be more appealing to searchers. In AdWords, your PPC ad will stand out even more with the addition of a third description line listing the searcher's city and state. More targeted, appealing ads means a higher clickthrough rate, which means a lower CPC in Google. Your ads will appear in local searches and in general search, and most engines will give you an enhanced listing as well. Choosing local search PPC can make you more visible everywhere, and more profitable everywhere as well.

The points made by the these analysts reinforce much of what we've already discussed in this book, but they also include some real gems of wisdom that you can take and start using in your online PPC campaigns, right now!

What about the future? Although we've talked some about upcoming trends, let's consolidate some of our knowledge and speculate a little on what might be just around the bend for pay-per-click advertising during the year 2007-2008 and beyond.

Chapter 13 – The Future of
Pay Per Click; Insights Into Upcoming Trends

When we look back on the last decade, it is difficult to believe the enormous growth the Internet has sustained, from its beginnings as a means for academics and government offices to communicate with each other to a full-fledged global marketplace. It took almost 40 years for television to achieve the same level of saturation among consumers that the Internet has achieved in a quarter of the time. One can only point to the power of this medium to attract and keep users attentive and entertained to explain such a massive implementation.

Like it or not, the Internet as a commercial enterprise is continuing (and will continue) to grow, mature, and expand. Considering that, the importance of creating a successful business presence online becomes more and more relevant—not necessarily to replace the "brick-and-mortar" setup of your physical place of business, but rather to complement it.

Small businesses traditionally have had more difficulty than larger companies in marketing themselves to consumers, relying mostly on word-of-mouth, location, small local advertising, or standardized ads in the yellow pages or community phone directories.

With the rise of online advertising, specifically in the search industry, this is changing. You are now able to reach qualified prospects and clients through the web, track your efforts to a tee, and aim to attract to your product clients whom you would never have considered possible to reach otherwise, due to the benefits of a global economy.

As you have learned throughout this book, pay-per-click marketing is a very lucrative opportunity for business owners and will continue to be so for years to come. New advertisers are starting to use pay per click, more people than ever before are using search engines, and everybody's trying to get onboard and take advantage of the available potential.

As we end our discussion of pay-per-click methods and tools, we wanted to share some predictions of what will happen in the near future in our industry.

The battle between the search engines is heating up. The past year (2006) started off with Google clearly in the lead and Yahoo! trailing far behind. However, several things have changed since then.

Yahoo! released their long-awaited update, dubbed Panama, as an upgrade to their old DirecTraffic center. Panama simulates the Google platform in the way that it targets and serves up ads, which is certainly an improvement over the last system. As with Google, the new Yahoo! system rewards smart advertisers who are more efficient with their ads, as that benefits everybody.

Microsoft entered the arena with their adCenter offering. According to many of their new advertisers, it is quite impressive in terms of features and traffic quality. Unfortunately, it is somewhat lacking in traffic volume, not being able to match the enormous market share currently enjoyed by Google. It is not an easy thing to switch a searcher's loyalty from Google or Yahoo! to Microsoft, so it remains to be seen how much of a market share Microsoft will gain in the coming years.

Taking into consideration the deep financial pockets of Microsoft, and their existing brand recognition, plus the fact that the majority of computers run on a Microsoft platform, it is certainly possible that they will succeed in making Microsoft Search a competitive product. It's up to them to step up to the plate and compete on the same level with their rivals.

Ask.com is also gaining ground, although it still has a long way to go to reach the status of the three giants of the industry.

A little bit of competition is good for everybody involved. It forces the search engines to improve themselves and it creates variety for advertisers, so not everybody winds up completely dependent on Google. Most importantly, it ultimately gives choice to users.

Sooner or later, AdWords and Yahoo! Search Marketing PPC products will become marketing techniques as well known and used as direct mail and telemarketing.

As that happens, we believe there will be an increasing switch from advertising media, such as TV and radio, to online advertising. We're not saying that TV and radio ads will disappear—we'll continue to see global, national, regional, and local companies on TV and radio, because these are still the best ways to promote a brand and reach millions of consumers quickly and efficiently.

Although it does seem that search engines want a piece of that as well. Google, for example, recently acquired dMarc Broadcasting (a radio advertising company) and seems to plan to enter that arena in the near future. On top of that, they are already testing newspaper and magazine advertisements on a limited scale with select advertisers. It seems as if they are looking for ways to duplicate offline what they've done online.

In any case, smaller companies, with tighter advertising budgets are becoming more aware of the less-expensive opportunities available to them via online advertising.

As more and more advertisers start to take advantage of the various pay-per-click options and enhancements being offered by search engines, several things may happen. For those advertisers who were around when the pay-per-click search engines debuted, they remember the "good old days" when quality keywords could be purchased for pennies. Now, the same keywords cost anywhere from 50 cents to several dollars per click, mainly as a result of more and more competition trying to get the same visitors.

The irony is that conversions of visitors to buyers hasn't really increased that much. When conversion rates improved, for the most part, improvements on the actual websites were responsible. The quality of the visitor for 5 cents per click five years ago is pretty much the same as the quality of the visitor that you pay $1 per click for today.

On top of that, one of the largest problems now is click fraud. As bid prices go up, there is more and more money to be made in click fraud. Fortunately, there has been some headway in this area with search engines, advertisers, and third-party click fraud monitoring companies coming together to try and develop standards on what exactly constitutes click fraud and how to combat it. The results are still yet to be seen, but this is certainly a step in the right direction.

Of course, click fraud will never fully be conquered, just as spam is still here and thriving, but with the proper tools, knowledge, and the support of search engines, advertisers will be able to minimize the effects of it.

As pay per click continues to increase in popularity, advertisers will need to become smarter and more efficient in order to keep a positive ROI and maintain their hard-fought-for keyword rankings. Google AdWords is setting the bar high with their Quality Score rating system that increases minimum bids for keywords that don't live up to the minimum standards. Yahoo! followed suit in their Panama update which also encourages smarter advertisers by giving them lower bid prices.

These techniques force advertisers to continuously improve their ads, improve their landing pages, improve their buying cycle, etc. If they don't, their ROI will fall and they may either be forced out of the largest available online search engines until they make sufficient changes to come back into their favor, or they will consider abandoning online advertising to their competitors—a move that few advertisers would willingly make.

However, if you do become better and better at crafting pay-per-click ads, this will not only benefit your PPC campaigns, but all of your other advertising techniques and your business in general. Granted, it's hard work and takes up a fair amount of time, but the results are worth it.

Search engines are currently in great competition to add new tools and new enhancements to their existing reports and bidding tools in order to attract new advertisers, as well as get advertisers to increase their spending with them.

Google is leading the pack in this respect. Over the last few years, they've done a lot on their end to provide advertisers with more options to manage their campaigns and also gained a lot of control over that information.

First, they began to offer Google Analytics—a powerful web analytics and tracking package—free of charge to all of their advertisers. By doing so, they provide the ability to analyze all of your incoming traffic and visitors and improve your ads based on that information.

Later on, they rolled out Google Checkout, a payment processor for Internet merchants. This has given their advertisers an option to process credit cards and rewarded them with low processing rates if they spent their marketing dollars on Google AdWords.

On one hand, it's a great deal for the advertiser. All these tools ultimately serve to benefit them. However, on the other hand, the advertiser may be providing a tad too much information to one of the largest sources of their traffic and sales or leads. Whether or not Google will use that information in ways advertisers had not anticipated is a question for the future.

One of the other growing trends is search beginning to move in several different directions. Of course, the classic model is still far in the lead, but as with all things, there are signs of evolution. Perhaps the most intriguing direction is in "social search."

Social search is still kind of a mystery. There isn't even one specific definition saying exactly what it is. In a nutshell, however, it's a kind of search where community and people determine the relevancy of the results.

For example, Google offers a service dubbed Co-op which allows people and companies to create custom search engines. A medical website can offer their users the technology of Google with the specialized knowledge and targeting that only they can offer by specifying which websites and which resources should be used in providing the results.

Social search is powerful because it puts the user in the driver's seat. Small groups of people or companies can play a role in search rather than a faceless conglomerate, and that kind of approach appeals to people in a way that standard search never can.

We also hope to see more improvements in local search and the mobile (cell phone) search businesses. Both of these are of tremendous benefit to smaller, local businesses that conduct most of their business with customers in person or over the phone.

Whether somebody is on a vacation and looking for a good restaurant or on a business trip and needs a 24-hour dry cleaning store, both local search and cell phone search capabilities deliver tremendous value to the consumer, who can search for local shops online in their hotel room or with the convenience of their cell phone.

One of the recent indicators of this trend is the deal inked by Yahoo! Local in early 2007 with Dash, an in-car navigation provider, to deliver Yahoo! Local content to end-users via the Dash interface. The system will automatically provide business information, whether it is concerning a restaurant or a store, based on the user's queries and GPS location. Currently, local business information is available through several other in-car and portable navigation systems. However, this seems to be the most advanced and versatile one so far.

Local businesses which have, for the most part, stayed out of the online world will soon see their competitors down the street reap the benefits of increased traffic (even without a website). These businesses will join in to compete for the increased business that will come as the convenience of local search becomes indispensable for consumers.

Unfortunately, we feel this means that print versions of the yellow page directories are doomed to eventual irrelevance to the majority of consumers, which will cut heavily into the revenues of these companies.

Most have already seen the writing on the wall, however, and have partnered with online services to offer online versions of their directories. They have also integrated paid advertising into their sites and are encouraging their traditional customers to try the online approach. It is both less costly and can be updated during the year if the business moves or changes their telephone number (both major disadvantages that have long been a problem for yellow page properties).

Signs indicate that the major yellow page properties are keeping up with the trend toward moving online and are offering new benefits to their advertisers and consumers. For those smaller entities that do not move into this market, tough times are surely ahead.

In the past couple of years, we haven't seen too much expansion into international online advertising from businesses in the United States and Canada. While most search engines do allow you to target specific countries, there needs to be a greater supply of quality traffic from other countries before this becomes truly effective.

Many countries are still behind in technology, with numerous complaints about the quality of search engine optimization companies just starting up in some parts of the world. The United Kingdom is already a major player, with some others on the European continent and in Scandinavia equally involved, but much of the rest of the world is still in the early stages of online development.

Within a few years, however, development of a quality online presence will become a fact of life in these countries in order to compete with the rest of the world for the global market and to provide the kind of local consumer experience that will become commonplace elsewhere. Asia, in particular, is exploding with all types of Internet-enabled technologies that are bound to impact the development of a greater online presence reaching further within, but also beyond, their own marketplace.

Of course, even targeting to different markets within the United States is also an enormous opportunity. The Hispanic market, for example, is growing incredibly fast and offers untapped potential for those companies that are willing to go through the trouble of addressing the specific needs of those users.

The world of pay per click has come a long way from its humble beginnings. Paid advertising online has come full circle—beginning as an accepted part of the online world, to being seen as an unnecessary and unwanted intrusion into the online experience by consumers, and back again to being a viewed by advertisers as a valuable way to "outwit, outplay, and outlast" (our apologies to the TV show "Survivor") their competitor. Consumers are accepting paid advertising of this type because, unlike popup ads, it does not interfere with their search experience. Those consumers in the know realize pay-per-click ads are a quick way to relevant results, especially when localization is added.

Pay-per-click advertising has taken much of the guesswork out of the consumer experience online, and we expect consumers to continue to see it as an opportunity to save time in their search for products and services, not just information.

Research shows that key consumer demographic groups are consistent online users and with the increasing pace of busy lifestyles, anything that will save time and effort in finding the right product for the right price at the right place (either through an online order or via local search for items people prefer to buy from local providers) is bound to succeed.

Our advice to you is to seriously consider investing in pay-per-click advertising in one or more of its various guises, as at least one part of your general marketing efforts. No advertiser should place all their efforts into one form of advertising, but the power of Internet marketing, particularly pay per click, cannot be ignored.

It can be a relatively low-investment opportunity that can, if handled with care, be an enormously profitable driver of business to your door. Growing numbers of consumers are compressing their day by "shopping" online during their workday and then stopping by the store they found online to purchase the product on the way home. Any small business that does not at least make an attempt to crack this marketplace will be left behind in the next couple of years.

One only needs to look at the behavior of younger consumers to see what lies ahead. Online marketing will continue to expand and diversify to meet the growing needs of a generation that has grown up with the Internet and whose behavior over the last couple of years clearly indicates the convenience and power of the Internet as a commercial enterprise. This marketing is attractive to them, and rapidly becoming the norm.

Don't be left behind! Use the techniques in this book and the advice offered by both us and the experts who contributed their thoughts to take advantage of this online commercial world—still a frontier in some ways, but rapidly becoming the sophisticated marketplace it is destined to be.

The final chapter of our book will give you information on how you can continue to be updated on developments in pay-per-click advertising. We will also make some final comments on further steps to take, including both print and online resources that can help you make your pay-per-click ad campaigns a success, whether this is your first attempt or you are a seasoned traveler of the pay-per-click environment.

Chapter 14 – Conclusion

As we come to the end of this book, it a good time to mention a few sources available to you for more advice and help in PPC advertising. We truly hope that you enjoyed reading and, most importantly, learned something useful from the book—whether you're a beginner or an experienced advertiser.

If you wish to learn more about this subject, there is a lot of quality literature available for you to peruse, some of which is identified in our Recommended Reading Appendix, as well as a number of excellent online resources listed in our Recommended Resources Appendix. We've also included a Glossary of common pay-per-click-related terms to help you along the way.

Will the future trends we predicted in the last chapter come to pass? We think there is a good possibility they will, but if there is one thing we have learned in our nine years of experience in the online advertising industry, is just when you think you have it figured out—wham! Something new comes along.

Advertisers need to stay up-to-date with what is happening in order to anticipate such moves and prepare for them. This book will be updated approximately every year with all the latest changes in the pay-per-click world. Existing customers will be eligible to receive the new book at a 15% discount in price at www.ppcbook.info/latest.

Pay-Per-Click Bonuses (as of March 2007)

Listed below are the special bonuses we promised our readers on the book's cover. These bonuses offer you credit at some of the leading pay-per-click engines and tools and are an excellent way to get started.

Yahoo!	$50 Bonus	www.ppcbook.info/yahoo
MIVA	$5 Bonus	www.ppcbook.info/miva
Search 123	$20 Bonus	www.ppcbook.info/search123
Kanoodle	$5 Bonus	www.ppcbook.info/kanoodle
Enhance	$25 Bonus	www.ppcbook.info/enhance
Mamma	$10 Bonus	www.ppcbook.info/mamma
SuperPages	$25 Bonus	www.ppcbook.info/superpages
Findology	$50 Bonus	www.ppcbook.info/findology
Search*feed*	Free Premium Service	www.ppcbook.info/searchfeed
ABCSearch	$100 Bonus	www.ppcbook.info/abcsearch

Another **FREE** bonus we'd like to offer you is a copy of the exclusive **"The Three Keys To Profitable Online Advertising"** report, written by W. Emerson Brantley III, an advertising guru with almost 30 years of marketing experience, who was among the first marketers to recognize the commercial potential of the Internet. The author combines traditional and new marketing techniques and explains how they apply to online advertising.

To download your **free** copy, simply go to www.mordcomm.com/report.pdf.

Appendix 1
Glossary

A-B Split Testing: Process of testing multiple landing pages or other components of your ads against each other to find which ones work better.

Affiliate: Typical term for a website that drives traffic to another website in exchange for a percent of sales from users driven to the site.

Auto Bidding: Tools or services that automatically adjust your bids to be just 1 cent more than your competitors. This helps avoid bid gaps and wasted money.

Backlink: Links found on other websites that will take the user to your website.

Bid: See *Keyword Bid.*

Bid Gap: Difference in bid prices between subsequent ads for the same keyword.

Broad Match: Originally a Google term, the phrase now is used commonly to refer to results from a keyword phrase that is very general in nature. For example, if a user searches for the phrase "leather recliners," and your PPC ad is of the broad match variety, the user will see results that include not just recliner ads, but also ads for leather, as well as results based solely on relevance to leather and/or recliners in general.

Click Fraud: Clicks on a PPC ad that are deliberately initiated with no interest in the content of the site or in investigating or purchasing a product, but whose sole intention is to deplete the PPC advertiser's account balance.

Cost Per Click (CPC): The amount you pay for each click on your ad. Some people use this term interchangeably with the pay-per-click cost.

Click-Through Rate (CTR): The percentage of people who click on a PPC ad out of the total number who see it. For example, if 100 people see your ad and 10 click on it, your CTR is 10%.

Contextual Ads: Advertising that is geared toward content. To catch the interest of the reader of the web page, your product or service must be highly related to the content at which they are looking. Contextual ads are typically found in content-rich sites, such as online newspapers, magazines, journals, and informational sites.

Conversion Rate: The percentage of visitors who are converted into buyers of your product/service. It is calculated as the number of clickthroughs divided by the number of actual conversions. The higher the conversion rate, the more effective your campaign has been.

CPM: The cost for 1,000 impressions or ad views.

Editorial Review: A process most PPC search engines require ads to undergo, whereby an employee checks your proposed PPC ad to ensure it fits the guidelines of the search engine in format, size, content, and sometimes other, often undisclosed, factors.

Exact Match: A Google term describing a keyword plan that will bring your ad up on results pages only if the searcher types the exact keyword phrase you have bid on. For example, if a user types in "leather recliners," only ads with those two words, in this exact order, will appear.

Fixed Bidding: A process by which you can specify a certain price you are willing to pay for a specific keyword, no matter how your competitors for that keyword change their bidding. Used in earlier times, PPC advertisers are now encouraged to use auto-bidding tools or manually adjust keyword bids to compete effectively.

Geo-Targeting: An option available on some PPC search engines that allows you to specify which countries the search engine reaches that you want your PPC ad to appear in.

Hits: The number of times a particular web page is viewed. The number of hits is independent of whether or not the same user is visiting the same page more than once. Sometimes referred to as *visits*.

Impression: Also known as *ad views*. "Impression" is the term used to describe the viewing of an ad by the user's browser.

Keyword: The terms that users enter into the search box of a search engine. Consequently, these are the word(s) you should choose to use in your pay-per-click campaign. Depending upon the company and the size of the campaign, the number of keywords used can range from a few to thousands.

Keyword Bid: The maximum amount of money you are prepared to pay every time a user clicks on your pay-per-click ad on a search engine, and thus visits your website.

Keyword Matching: Means of organizing or allocating your keywords so that your ad only appears when a user types in a certain combination of your keywords. See *Broad Match*, *Exact Match*, and *Phrase Match*.

Landing Page: The page you choose to have searchers taken to when they click on your pay-per-click ad. The landing page need not be your homepage and, in fact, is usually a page that is designed specifically to sell your product.

Local Search: The ability to search for results by location. Depending on the search engine, local search capabilities can be limited to geo-tracking (see *Geo-Tracking*) or may go as far as searching by region, city/town, zip code, or postal code.

Minimum Bid: The minimum amount required by a pay-per-click search engine for either a specific keyword, type of keyword, or the overall minimum bid acceptable for any keyword.

Negative Keywords: Keywords that limit the appearance of your ad if they are including in the search phrase. For example, if you are bidding on "web hosting," you may want to include the word "free" as a negative keyword. Your ad will therefore not appear if a search is made for "free web hosting."

Organic Listings: Regular search results that appear when a browser user types in a particular keyword or keyword phrase. Organic listings include links to pages on your website that either you have submitted directly to the search engine, or that the search engine's robot has crawled on your site.

Page Views: The number of times a web page is viewed.

Paid Inclusion: A sales technique currently under review by many search engines, paid inclusion is where an advertiser arranges to pay a search engine a certain amount of money to ensure a ranking in their search results. Most search engines do not guarantee the ranking will be among the highest. Many search engines have either stopped this type of plan or are in the process of considering removing this option for online marketing.

Pay-Per-Click (PPC) Advertising: A method of marketing where a business pays a certain amount of money each time someone clicks on a small ad on a search engine's results page or homepage and is then taken to the advertiser's website.

Pay-Per-Click Search Engine (PPCSE): A search engine that offers pay-per-click advertising as an option to businesses.

Pay Per Performance™ Web Search: The first PPC product from Overture, which debuted in 1998.

Phrase Match: A Google keyword strategy (now becoming known as such on many different search engines) that produces search results that only include the entire phrase, in the order in which the words are placed. This type of match would bring up results that only relate to "leather recliners," for example. It would also show results for "brown leather recliners," because the phrase words are together, but not for searches for "leather type recliners," where the words are out of sequence.

Relevance: The degree to which a search result or a PPC ad matches the search terms the user put in the search box. Relevance is not only key to a satisfactory search result for your visitors, but is increasingly a factor in search engines' deciding on how organic listings are sorted.

Return On Investment (ROI): The bottom line; that is, the amount of money you make compared to the amount of money you have spent. Many tools exist to help you calculate your ROI for whatever undertaking, including pay-per-click campaigns.

Search Engine Marketing (SEM): Activities designed to increase the ranking of your website in search engines. Such activities include pay-per-click advertising and regular search engine optimization.

Search Engine Optimization (SEO): A variety of techniques whereby you change the content, keywords, meta tags, placement of text versus code, etc., in order to enhance your ranking in a search engine.

SEMPO: Acronym for the Search Engine Marketing Professional Organization at http://www.sempo.org/.

Unique Visitor: The number of people who visit a web page. If one person visits the same web page three or four times, the statistics will list them as one unique visitor.

Appendix 2
Recommended Reading

Call to Action: Secret Formulas to Improve Online Results
by Bryan Eisenberg, Jeffrey Eisenberg, Lisa T. Davis

ISBN: 078521965X, October 2006, 288 pp.

Price: $24.99

Pay Per Click Search Engine Marketing for Dummies
by Peter Kent

ISBN: 0471754943, February 2006, 368 pp.

Price: $24.99

Google Advertising Guerrilla Tactics: Google Advertising A-Z Plus 150 Killer AdWords Tips & Tricks
by Editors of BottleTree Books LLC

ISBN: 1933747013, March 2006, 216 pp.

Price: $24.98

Winning Results with Google AdWords
by Andrew Goodman

ISBN: 0072257024, July 2005, 376 pp.

Price: $24.99

Make Easy Money with Google: Using the AdSense Advertising Program
by Eric Giguere

ISBN: 0321321146, June 2005, 272 pp.

Price: $24.99

Google Advertising Tools: Cashing in with AdSense, AdWords, and the Google APIs
by Harold Davis

ISBN: 0596101082, January 2006, 353 pp.

Price: $29.99

Ultimate Guide to Google AdWords
by Perry Marshall and Bryan Todd

ISBN: 1599180308, November 2006, 304 pp.

Price: $24.95

Search Engine Advertising: Buying Your Way to the Top to Increase Sales
by Catherine Seda

ISBN: 0735713995, February 2004, 368 pp.
Price: $29.99

Search Engine Visibility
by Shari Thurow

ISBN: 0735712565, December 2002, 320 pp.

Price: $34.99

Ultra-Advanced Seminar on Google AdWords
by Jason Potash, Perry Marshall, and Don Crowther

URL: **www.ppcbook.info/googleadvanced**

Price: $99

Google AdWords Handbook: 21 Ways to Maximize Results
by Andrew Goodman

URL: **www.ppcbook.info/handbook**

Price: $69

Appendix 3
Recommended Resources

PayPerClickUniverse.com

PayPerClickUniverse is a free resource providing unbiased information to the small-to-medium-sized business owner interested in exploring the world of pay-per-click advertising (PPC). Offers periodic reviews of search engines and tools, as well as a free newsletter, a blog, a search engine marketing news feed, and various special offers for PPC advertising.

PayPerClickSearchEngines.com

Based in Australia, this newly redesigned website offers a lot of information—reviews sorted into different categories (including a separate section for UK-based PPC search engines), a newsletter, articles, and a variety of other information for PPC advertisers.

SearchEngineWatch.com

As part of the ClickZ network, this website offers a huge amount of information on every aspect of search engines imaginable, including pay per click. News, informative articles, extensive forums, as well as a "members-only" area, have made this website a standard source for up-to-date information (not only on search engines, but on how users are reacting to changes in the industry.

SearchEngineLand.com

The new home of Danny Sullivan, Greg Sterling, Chris Sherman, Barry Schwartz and others, SearchEngineLand has a blog on search-related news that is one of the best online. Straightforward, unbiased discussion of current issues and how the latest changes at Google, Yahoo! etc., are bound to affect you.

SearchEngineForums.com

A collection of forums all related to search engines in one way or another, this site has a wide assortment of topics to choose from, including an extensive pay-per-click selection, with separate forums for many of the major PPC search engines.

EndOfClickFraud.com

From the designers of AdWatcher, this website has a neat little tool that will estimate how much money you could be losing to click fraud, as well as offering information on the extent of the problem and a solution in their tracking software.

TopRankBlog.com

A blog all on its own, TopRankBlog also is home to the extremely interesting Search Marketing Blogs list, a collection of more than 320 blogs on search marketing that is updated each week. A great resource for finding out which blogs are hot and which are not, and what each concentrates on to make choosing which blogs will fit best with your needs.

Search Engine Marketing and Pay-Per-Click Blogs

There are literally hundreds of relevant and useful blogs online today that deal with search engine marketing and/or pay-per-click topics. Here is a list of some of the blogs that are particularly suited to PPC advertising. This is by no means an exhaustive list and many excellent blogs exist that deal with the larger topic of search engine marketing (see above entry for access to a good list of SEM-related blogs to track down the latest and the greatest).

Ask.com Blog—the official blog from search engine Ask has good interviews and a monthly run-down of Ask Answers at blog.ask.com.

Britopian Marketing Blog—marketing blog from the UK loaded with lots of info on paid search, social media and search engine news that is just as useful to US advertisers at www.britopian.com.

eWhisper.net—Brad Geddes talks about a lot of search topics, but specializes in PPC topics and issues as well at www.ewhisper.net.

Google Analytics Blog—all the news and tips from the Google team in Analytics at analytics.blogspot.com.

Google Webmaster Central—although this blog deals with a lot more than PPC (AdWords), there are PPC gems throughout at googlewebmastercentral.blogspot.com.

GotAds—mostly concerned with Google and Yahoo! (but who isn't?) at gotads.blogspot.com.

Inside AdWords—the official word on Google and a must-read at adwords.blogspot.com.

Jonathan Mendez's Blog—nice focus on branding and search at www.optimizeandprophesize.com.

Paul Jahn's Local Search Blog—mostly focused on local search marketing trends with a Minnesota focus at localmn.wordpress.com.

JenSense Making Sense of Contextual Advertising—a must-read for contextual advertisers at www.jensense.com.

Mike The Internet Guy—a blog with an emphasis on local search, both in terms of SEO and paid advertising at www.miketheinternetguy.com/blog/.

PPC Blog—subtitled "A cynical look at Pay Per Click," this blog is based in the UK and has some great tips and info that all advertisers can find useful at www.ppcblog.co.uk.

Search Marketing Standard Blog—although covering all aspects of SEO, Garrett French blogs about paid advertising news and issues as well at www.searchmarketingstandard.com/blog/.

Search Engine Roundtable puts together forum listings from all the major online forums and digests them into readable entries at www.seoroundtable.com.

The SEO Coach is Dan Thies blog on search engine marketing tips, strategy and tactics from a keyword research specialist at www.seoresearchlabs.com/blog.

ShoeMoney—a blog by Jeremy Shoemaker that concentrates on how you can make more money online with advertising at www.shoemoney.com.

Small Business SEM—blog about many topics related to smaller businesses, with a nice local search marketing guide as well as local search blog entries at www.smallbusinesssem.com.

SponsoredB2B—fairly recent entry into the discussion on B2B marketing via PPC at sponsoredb2b.blogspot.com/.

Tech Mentat—blog from Kris Keimig of LookSmart with some good info on PPC located at www.techmentat.com.

Yahoo! Search Marketing Blog—the official Yahoo! blog on search engine marketing located at ysmblog.com.

As stated earlier, this is by no means an exhaustive list (even of the PPC-centered blogs out there) but it's a place to start. Check out the blogs that your favorite bloggers read and you'll soon work up a list of your own that you can sign up for a feed from.

SEOBook.com

In addition to providing a great SEO blog, SEOBook has access to a ton of free search engine optimization tools. Specific tools to fit the pay-per-click advertiser's needs include a bunch of keyword research tools, one specifically designed by site owner Aaron Wall himself.

SplitTester.com

Split Tester is an interesting, free tool that will compare two ads, using "statistical significance" to project the long-term success of your ads based on early clickthrough rates.

Google AdWords Resources
https://adwords.google.com/select/library

Google.com offers a lot of information for pay-per-click advertisers using the AdWords (and AdSense) programs, including an extremely comprehensive FAQ section for quick answers to specific questions. Information is provided for international advertisers, but the majority is geared toward the US market. If you like to do your reading offline, there is a print option to print out all the FAQs from every AdWords help page (https://adwords.google.com/support/).

The online demos and in-depth, text-based guides walk you step-by-step through all aspects of the AdWords program. The available material covers beginning and managing an AdWords campaign, and includes information on all the tools available to help you manage your campaigns.

Yahoo! Advertiser Resources
http://searchmarketing.yahoo.com/rc/srch/

SearchMarketing.Yahoo.com also has a lot of information on their website to help you set up and manage your PPC advertising, for both US and international advertisers. The main area to begin with for US advertisers is the Advertiser Center. An "Advertiser Workbook" is available to download and an area called "Yahoo! Search Marketing 101" introduces you to the PPC ad program. There are many interactive tutorials available, especially about some of the free tools offered, which include:

Keyword Suggestion Tool - Lets you check five generic terms for your website, and the traffic they receive on this search engine.

http://inventory.overture.com/d/searchinventory/suggestion/

ROI Calculator - Allows you to instantly see if you are making a profit from your PPC campaign, simply by plugging in a few numbers. You can also download this tool if you have Microsoft Excel, so it is always available on your desktop.

http://www.content.overture.com/d/USm/learning/roitop.jhtml

It is rumored that the free tools will disappear from the site as the Panama update progresses, but the keyword suggestion tool is such a hallmark of Yahoo! that it seems likely they will be preserved in some fashion, if only for advertisers themselves.

Final Message From the Authors

Final Message From the Authors (MordComm, Inc.)

 The "Pay-Per-Click Search Engine Marketing Handbook" was written by Boris and Eugene Mordkovich, founders of MordComm Inc., a New York City-based firm that develops services to help entrepreneurs and small businesses advertise effectively on the Internet.

It was later updated in 2007 with the latest industry updates, strategies and advice.

If you have any questions or comments about this book, or about online advertising in general, you can contact the authors directly by emailing them at book@mordcomm.com. Don't be surprised if you hear back from them the same day!

MordComm, Inc. has developed several other tools and resources for online advertising campaigns, including a bid manager, a click-fraud tracking and detection tool, and an affordable PPC management and tracking tool, among others.

Check out the next few pages for details on all MordComm products, including their highly successful Search Marketing Standard print magazine.

Search Marketing Standard Magazine – Print Publication
www.SearchMarketingStandard.com

Search Marketing Standard is the first magazine that search marketers can call their own. The ever-growing demand for search marketing services and information has led to a need for a specialized magazine dedicated to making this knowledge accessible.

At Search Marketing Standard we've stepped up to the challenge and set out to create the first publication for the search marketing industry.

Search Marketing Standard is devoted completely to the world of search marketing. It covers pay per click advertising, search engine optimization, web analytics, click fraud, local and contextual search, and other search-related topics.

Each publication features articles and advice from leading experts in the field, interviews with the who's-who of the industry, reviews of the most popular tools and services, latest news and trends, and much more.

A yearly subscription to the magazine starts at just $15 for four issues for US-based readers and $20 for international subscribers (shipping included).

Whether you are a professional search marketer on a quest to improve your knowledge and expertise or a business owner trying to take advantage of the great potential search advertising has to offer, you will find the information you need in Search Marketing Standard magazine.

Get a subscription at www.SearchMarketingStandard.com

AdWatcher – Click Fraud Monitor and Ad Tracker
www.AdWatcher.com

AdWatcher is an all-in-one tool that helps you **manage your pay-per-click advertising**, **track your Return On Investment** (ROI), and **monitor your ad campaigns for fraudulent activity**. It will help you monitor all of your pay-per-click search engine campaigns from one convenient location and will tell you exactly what works and what doesn't.

We would like to offer you a chance to try out our software **for 30 days absolutely free**. Of course, even if you decide to stay with us after the initial 30 days you will still be able to cancel and get a complete refund for up to 90 days, no questions asked.

Still not convinced? There are **several reasons** why you should give AdWatcher a try:

1) AdWatcher will track all of your ad campaigns and will tell you **exactly what works** and **what doesn't**. If you're spending money on ads and they don't convert, wouldn't you want to know about it?

2) According to CNET, up to **20% of all pay-per-click traffic is fraudulent**. AdWatcher will not only monitor your traffic, but will alert you of any fraudulent activity and will help you get refunds back from the search engines.

3) Only AdWatcher offers a **built-in A/B Split Testing** capability, which allows you to test multiple landing pages simultaneously to check which ones convert better. By simply changing a headline or a color, you can double your conversion rates. We can help you improve your sales process simply and painlessly.

AdWatcher comes with a **<u>100% Money Back</u>** and **<u>200% ROI Performance Increase</u>** guarantees. Plus, we offer **free installation** and **live support**. We want to make your experience with us is as easy and satisfying as possible and we're willing to go the extra mile to do that.

Sign up for the free 30-day trial today at <u>www.AdWatcher.com</u>

AdScientist – Pay-Per-Click Bid Manager
www.AdScientist.com

AdScientist is the ultimate pay-per-click bid management and optimization software that helps you manage your keyword bids in major pay-per-click search engines (Google, Yahoo! and Microsoft adCenter) and many others, such as MIVA (FindWhat), Epilot, 7Search, Enhance Interactive, Lycos, BrainFox, Searchfeed, and Kanoodle (Pulse360).

Managing your online advertising campaigns can be a time consuming and difficult process. Save yourself time and money by using AdScientist. It will help you build your keyword list, manage your keywords, automatically monitor your keyword bids and URLs at all major pay-per-click search engines, notify you of your current bids, analyze your ranking positions and fix bid gaps.

We would like to offer you a chance to try out our software for 30 days absolutely free. Of course, even if you decide to stay with us after the initial 30 days you will still be able to cancel and get a complete refund for up to 90 days, no questions asked.

AdScientist comes with a 100% Money Back guarantee. We want to make your experience with us as easy and satisfying as possible and we're willing to go the extra mile to do that.

Sign up today at www.AdScientist.com

PayPerClickUniverse – Everything You Need to Know About PPC
www.PayPerClickUniverse.com

PayPerClickUniverse is a free, unbiased, informational site concentrating on every aspect of pay-per-click advertising. In our fourth year online, PayPerClickUniverse is the site of choice for unbiased information that users can trust.

Through PayPerClickUniverse, we provide periodic reviews of search engines and the latest PPC tools, a free monthly newsletter, a resource area filled with relevant articles, tips, interviews, all the latest news in the industry, special offers from selected search engines, a blog from top executives at MordComm, Inc., as well as a number of additional resources.

Whether you're just getting started or consider yourself to be an experienced advertiser, we encourage you to bookmark PayPerClickUniverse and use it as your portal to the latest updates and changes in the industry. We invite you to visit, look through the website, and feel free to contact us via PayPerClickUniverse with any questions or comments regarding pay-per-click advertising.

Visit www.PayPerClickUniverse.com and get an additional $300 worth of pay-per-click credits!

Printed in the United States
92051LV00005B/133-135/A

9 781411 628175